"When well-published psychological researchers and cognitive behavioral pioneers such as Drs. Art and Christine Maguth Nezu address the issue of spirituality, we have to listen! In many ways the ideas are not simply about building self-esteem, but rather, without freeing the individual to move in a number of new, possibly risky, directions and enter new situations. This will build a greater sense of self-efficacy more than anything else. The book is well-written, as we have come to expect from this articulate pair. The book is, in itself, a gift."

—Art Freeman, professor and chair, department of psychology, Philadelphia College of Osteopathic Medicine

"I have searched for a self-help book to recommend to my clients that would provide an integration of psychological and spiritual techniques that they could apply to their own life development. *Awakening Self-Esteem* provides a clear roadmap for the journey of awakening and enhanced well-being that can be followed by anyone who wishes to travel along this path. Based on principles of mindfulness and lifestyle balance, the material in this book contains specific guidelines and opportunities for practice that are both challenging and exciting in their scope. Overall, this is a journey of adventure and discovery, and is well worth the trip!"

—G. Alan Marlatt, Ph.D., professor and director, Addictive Behaviors Research Center, University of Washington, department of psychology.

awakening self-esteem

Spiritual and Psychological Techniques to Enhance Your Well-Being

CHRISTINE MAGUTH NEZU, PH.D., ABPP
ARTHUR M. NEZU, PH.D., ABPP
FOREWORD BY E. THOMAS DOWD, PH.D.

New Harbinger Publications, Inc.

Distributed in Canada by Raincoast Books

Copyright © 2003 by Christine Maguth Nezu and Arthur M. Nezu
New Harbinger Publications, Inc.
5674 Shattuck Avenue
Oakland, CA 94609

Cover design by Amy Shoup
Edited by Carole Honeychurch
Text design by Tracy Marie Carlson

ISBN 1-57224-343-0 Paperback

New Harbinger Publications' Web site address: www.newharbinger.com

05   04   03

10   9   8   7   6   5   4   3   2   1

First printing

This book is dedicated to all the souls among us who have the courage to embark on a spiritual journey.

Contents

PART I
Spirituality and Self-Esteem:
Preparing For The Journey

PART II
Journey Destinations: Spiritual Goals

Foreword

I am very pleased to be asked to write the foreword for Drs. Christine and Arthur Nezu's new book. As an ordained minister and a board-certified psychologist, I am acutely aware of the importance both spiritual health and mental health play in a person's overall physical and emotional health. Like love and marriage, it's difficult to have one without the other.

However, it is only recently that professional psychology has recognized the importance of spirituality and religion in people's lives. Some of the seminal figures in psychology have even argued that religion especially is essentially a form of neuroticism. Yet the literature indicates that religious people are more psychologically (and even physically) healthy, not less. But this literature has historically been relegated to the periphery of the profession. Only in the last few years has there been a series of books and articles in the mainstream literature dealing with the psychology of religion and psychotherapy with religious and spiritual persons.

The timing is therefore perfect for Chris and Art's new book. Their five spiritual destinations—enriching relationships, fostering acceptance, learning to forgive, increasing patience, and creating hope—are central to both psychological and spiritual health. Both psychology and religion/spirituality have an increase in self-esteem as a goal. I am impressed with the exercises they have created to help readers on their spiritual and self-esteem journey and the rich detail they've included. They have used the best knowledge in the psychological field—mindfulness meditation, visualization exercises, autogenic training—to help the readers awaken and improve their own self-esteem. The numerous case examples will provide readers with applications to their own lives.

The focus is on spirituality rather than religion as such—a wise decision in my estimation. Too often we focus on the specifics of what I have come to call "brand-name religions" and lose the essence in the process. Spirituality transcends religion although, in my experience, religion at its best can aid us significantly in developing our spiritual life.

Anyone can profit from this book! It is not necessary to have low self-esteem for it to be enhanced. It's not necessary to begin from a spiritual "ground zero" for spirituality to be enhanced—but a reader with no spiritual life risks being drawn to one by this book. One need not belong to any of the world's great religions to benefit. One need only approach this book with an open mind and a willing heart. If you do, you will benefit greatly.

—Rev. E. Thomas Dowd, Ph.D., ABPP
Interim Chair, Department of Psychology
Kent State University

Acknowledgments

This book began as many good ideas do—as a spirited conversation over a cup of coffee, this time with New Harbinger's editor Catherine Sutker. As such, it seems appropriate to begin with Catherine as the first person to acknowledge and extend our thanks. It was she who had the faith in us to put our ideas on paper. In addition, the collective expertise of everyone at New Harbinger has helped nurture our original effort into the final manuscript. The final draft was greatly aided by Carole Honeychurch's gifted editorial hand.

We would also like to thank all those people who have influenced our thinking, helped us with our own spiritual goals and psychological insights, and contributed to our desire to write this book.

We especially acknowledge our personal friends, the Reverend Mandy Derr, the Reverends Drs. Dave and Suzan Farley, and Dr. Tom Dowd, for their patience and participation in the many philosophical, psychological, and spiritually-focused conversations we have had over the years.

We would also like to acknowledge the collective patients in both of our psychology practices who have often been beacons of courage and dared to let their human spirits overcome difficult childhoods, stressful life situations, and devastating losses.

Finally, we wish to acknowledge and appreciate the challenges and problems we have each faced in our own lives, particularly those challenges faced by the creation of our family. Along with our laughter and joy, our life paths have also included the healing of emotional wounds, recovery from loss, and transcending racial prejudice. We have come to trust the love and spiritual connection we have for each other, as well as with Frank, Ali, and Linda. This is certainly a demonstrable example of how the marriage of spirits and character can transcend life difficulties and grow with change.

Our sincere gratitude for these, as well as all the gifts, of this life.

Introduction

Every second is of infinite value
—Goethe

What Will You Do with the Rest of Your Life?

What a question to contemplate! Will you try to answer this question with your head? With your heart? Or both? Is this query exciting or scary? Is it your first impulse to avoid thinking about such a question and put this book down immediately? Or will you continue reading with eager anticipation, in search of guidance to address such a question?

To help you think about your answer, sit back and picture an imaginary clock—a large, digital clock.

The Imaginary Clock

Take a slow, deep breath and imagine that you're looking at a large, digital clock, the kind that you often see on billboards. It's the kind that you saw a few years ago, right before all of the millennium celebrations, the type of clock where you can watch every second, and then every minute, pass by. Close your eyes and imagine such a clock now. See the large, red, digital numbers on a black background. Try to envision the seconds turning into minutes and the minutes into hours. The turning is constant, and at times feels relentless—you can't stop it.

Now, imagine that these changing numbers represent the passing moments in your lifetime.

As you picture this clock, what comes to mind? Do you, like some people, feel a sense of urgency to complete various tasks at home and work? Are you concerned about the time you've wasted, looking back with regret over failed goals and yearning for the things that you still want out of life? Perhaps you experience a feeling of resignation, thinking that life is too short and in order to accomplish what you had hoped you may have to compromise your dreams. Maybe you feel that you don't have what it takes to accomplish your goals. Maybe you have some self-doubts and question your abilities to get what you want out of life.

In reaction to this image of passing time, many people have told us that they experience some negative feelings. Some have expressed fears of the future; others even report that they are frightened at the prospect of death. Many become very concerned about all the things they want to do in so short a time, but feel stuck and unable to move. Other people envision themselves at a huge crossroad, with numerous paths ahead of them but no signs to guide them as to the best direction to take. Still others only see huge obstacles standing in their way, blocking their ability to move forward.

Alternatively, there are people who have told us that they are actually energized by such a question and become very curious about what the next moment, day, week, or year will present in the way of new learning experiences. They feel joyful about the unknown experiences they have yet to encounter and the people they have yet to meet.

Self-Esteem and the Future

As you can see, the image of the clock inspires very different thoughts and feelings about the future in different people. Most psychologists would agree that our views or thoughts about the future can be greatly affected by our view of ourselves. In other words, the way we think and feel about ourselves, our abilities, our self-worth—that is, our self-esteem—can affect the way we think and feel about the future.

Self-esteem is made up of what we think and feel about ourselves. Unfortunately, we can fall into the trap of comparing ourselves to others and derive our self-esteem based on the reputation we have among other people. This leads to thinking about and evaluating ourselves in relationship to other people. Are we better than most? As good as our next-door neighbor? As smart as our coworkers? As attractive as other family members or friends? How we feel and think about ourselves greatly affects the goals we set for ourselves and what we do to reach (or foil) those goals. If our self-esteem is solid and we are at peace with who we are and unconcerned about how we stack up against everyone else, then it's likely that we view the future with anticipation and joy while trying to savor each passing moment. On the other hand, if we feel self-doubt, constantly questioning our ability to reach our goals, then the future feels like a minefield, chock full of potential problems and obstacles waiting to explode in our faces.

Once again, reflect upon the imaginary clock and take a moment to experience the feelings associated with your thoughts. Take that moment now.

What feelings come up? Perhaps you view the constantly changing numbers as evidence of how everything in life continually changes. If so, you may look forward with excitement to the new opportunities that can be explored and appreciated with each passing moment. On the other hand, perhaps you view the constantly changing numbers with trepidation and concern, fearing that time is running out and you will be unable to find happiness, peace, and a sense of well-being. If you'd rather face the future with hope, excitement, and an expectation that you'll find happiness, read on.

Who Is This Book For?

This book is for people who question their ability to find happiness in the future, persons confused as to whether they will ever feel a sense of balance, harmony, and peace. Perhaps this describes you. You may be feeling lost and not quite on track concerning your future goals. Maybe you often feel plagued by self-doubt and have a lowered sense of your self-worth. Your confidence in your abilities to find such balance is limited and you wish to enhance your self-esteem in order to have a more positive future and improve your overall sense of well-being. Alternatively, although you may be in a good relationship now or feel that work is going okay, there continues to be a nagging feeling that something is missing. You may feel sad, alone, out of sync with the world, or searching for answers.

If any of these feelings describe you, this book can help. On one hand, it provides a set of specific life-changing tools that have been scientifically shown to be effective in enhancing self-esteem, improving one's quality of life, and enhancing well-being (for example, decreasing feelings of depression, anxiety, hopelessness, and loneliness). However, this is not just another book on enhancing self-esteem. Note that the title is *Awakening Self-Esteem*. We chose the word "awakening" deliberately because of the different context in which we present and discuss these self-help strategies—that is, within a framework that recognizes and attempts to foster the important healing powers provided by one's own spirituality.

Taking a Spiritual Journey to Awaken Self-Esteem

This book represents a journey—a spiritual journey. It provides both a set of destinations and the means by which to reach them. Each of the five destinations represents a spiritual goal. The sixth and final destination is awakening your self-esteem. The book is set up such that each place, in and of itself, is an important and worthwhile place to go to. In other words, it may be an important spiritual goal for you to reach. Moreover, each goal allows you to take a step closer to awakening your self-esteem. The actual journey to each destination further involves learning a set of skills that are invaluable tools for living (for example, changing negative thinking, learning to relax, and seeking help from a Higher Power). As such, the journey itself to each destination is potentially life-changing. These tools are also geared to help improve your quality of life by decreasing feelings of distress, improving your skills to cope with difficult problems, and enhancing your ability to reach your spiritual goals more capably.

> When a man does not know what harbor he is making for, no wind is the right wind.
>
> —Seneca

Because each destination is meaningful in and of itself, you can seek each goal in any order that you wish. This means that, after you read chapters 2 and 3, which will prepare you for your journey, you can jump ahead to any desired chapter when you want to. However, reaching each destination and learning how to use all the various life tools described within each journey helps you to achieve the ultimate destination of awakening your self-esteem more readily and meaningfully. In other words, by going through each smaller journey along the way and stopping at every destination, the ultimate goal of awakening your self-esteem will become more accessible and will feel richer and more complete. Achieving each goal will enhance the process of eventually awakening your self-esteem. But it's really up to you on how to plan such a journey. No matter which path you take, we'll be there to help.

What Are the Destinations?

Chapters 2 and 3 help prepare you for this journey. Specifically, chapter 2 helps you make the first steps on the journey, as well as aiding you to develop your journey itinerary. Because one needs to be awake while traveling in order to enjoy and get the most out of this particular journey, chapter 3 helps to foster your spiritual awareness. Here we provide tools to maximize your ability to "see" and experience the journey in a way that's sharper, clearer, and unobstructed. As such, reading these two chapters is very important before you embark on your travels.

The five destinations, or spiritual goals, are as follows:

« Enhancing relationships (chapter 3)

« Fostering acceptance (chapter 4)

« Learning to forgive (chapter 5)

« Increasing patience (chapter 6)

« Creating hope (chapter 7)

The final destination, awakening self-esteem, can be found in chapter 8.

Note that this book is not intended to provide "spiritual advice," per se. Although we borrow quotes and ideas from many spiritual leaders throughout the centuries, we leave advice to the wisdom of the scholars in each reader's chosen spiritual tradition. Rather, we provide a structured journey to help you reach the spiritual goals that are important to you.

Do You Need a Specific Religion?

Definitely not. A review of the wide range of traditional and contemporary approaches to spirituality reveals that there are central or core messages common across most religions and spiritual philosophies. These include messages of love, acceptance, compassion, forgiveness, a commitment to help others, a sense of purpose, surrender to a higher power, and the experience of personal peace. This common spiritual language translates into important spiritual goals for many people, irrespective of their religious beliefs. When people work toward such goals, progress toward enhancing their self-esteem is an inevitable outcome. The reason for this may be rooted in the idea that as we progress toward our spiritual goals, we are able to see ourselves as a meaningful and purposeful part of the universe. As such, awakening self-esteem is a very important part of our spirituality.

Given the commonality of such core themes across traditional and nontraditional religions, it's likely that people of varying faiths, including those who don't belong to any formal religious organization, will find this journey meaningful. Note that this book concerns itself with *spiritual* goals, broadly defined.

What is Spirituality?

Spirituality is concerned with individual subjective experiences. It does not necessarily involve formal religion, although for many people it certainly does. Coming from this perspective, especially as it relates to the type of journey contained in this book, we define spirituality as an individualized view of the world that is both inward-focused (acknowledging our own value and worth) and outward-focused (acknowledging that there is something greater than ourselves in the world). Psychologists Bill Miller and Carl Thoresen (1999) define the *goal* of spirituality as "the alleviation of mental, emotional, and spiritual distress thought to be at least in part caused by the lack of an appropriate relationship with ultimate reality" (p. 20).

"Ultimate reality" for some may represent a particular Higher Power or deity, such as God in the Judeo-Christian faiths or Allah in the Moslem faith. For others, that ultimate reality can be nature, as in the Japanese Shinto belief system. For still others, it can be the sense that we are all part of the same universal energy. In any case, because spirituality is so often uniquely and individually defined, we will not impose our definition on you, but rather leave it up to you to define your own sense of spiritual beliefs. The journey we provide will therefore be relevant to anyone with a set of spiritual beliefs, regardless of how such beliefs are defined.

How Will This Book Awaken Your Self-Esteem?

In order to better understand how spiritual goals are an important path to self-esteem, it makes sense to look at the meaning behind such words. The term "spirit" is often defined as the animating principle of life or one's "vital essence." A "goal" is defined as an achievement toward which effort is directed. Putting these definitions together, *spiritual goals can involve directing our efforts to discover our vital essence.* Most spiritual belief systems propose that this basic essence is present in each and every one of us, connected to each other and to an eternal source of love and energy—a Higher Power, so to speak. Many different words are used to describe this vital essence that is always present and waiting to be discovered. These include terms such as "light," "energy," "inner life," "true self," or "soul." Regardless of the actual words we use, when we are in touch with this wonderful and mysterious part of ourselves, our experiences are richer, our choices are more confident, and most important, our self-esteem is awakened. As noted earlier, when describing the resulting increase in self-esteem, we have chosen to use the term "awakened," rather than "achieved" or "developed." This is intentional because your spiritual essence is *already present*, waiting to be awakened by you. Think of it as peeling off all the various layers of negative thinking and feelings that have only served to obscure your view, thus finally allowing you to see and experience your vital essence.

The Challenge of Spiritual Goals

Spiritual discovery and transformation requires work. While there are many excellent readings available by various religious leaders regarding spiritual themes, seldom is a "how to" manual provided that can serve as useful and practical guides for people seeking such goals. For example, although teachings from a spiritual leader may inspire people to learn to forgive or seek peace, how they actually go about accomplishing such goals can be a very challenging task. As such, it's possible that the journey to such destinations can become very difficult, confusing, and hard to accomplish, regardless of how much one wants to get there. As psychologists, we know that by learning to use a set of practical and well-tested self-change strategies, you can reach your goals more readily. We believe that blending psychological science and spiritual goals can be a very powerful combination of efforts that can help you to actually realize your spiritual goals, and by doing so, awaken your self-esteem.

Some of you might wonder how two such seemingly different ways of understanding the world can work together. Consider a quote by Albert Einstein, whom you know as one of the greatest scientists who ever lived: "Science without religion is lame; religion without science is blind." In essence, he was strongly suggesting that both religion, or spirituality, and science are inextricably tied together—one without the other is actually lessened and compromised.

Current scientific thinking is increasingly providing evidence in support of such a tenet. Consider the following:

※ Research by neuroscientist Richard Davidson indicates that people who engaged in a eight-week course in mindfulness meditation, a form of Zen Buddhist meditation practice, not only reduced their anxiety, but improved their immune systems and increased the activity in the area of the brain associated with positive emotions, such as joy, enthusiasm, and good will (Goleman 2003).

※ Many scientific studies have found that religious involvement and spirituality are associated with better health outcomes, including greater longevity, coping skills, and health-related quality of life, as well as less anxiety, depression, and suicide. For example, a study involving over ten thousand male Israeli civil servants found that Orthodox Jewish men had a 20 percent decreased risk of fatal coronary heart disease compared with nonreligious men after controlling for age, blood pressure, smoking, diabetes, and weight (Friedlander, Kark, and Stein 1986).

※ Neuroscientists Andrew Newberg and Eugene D'Aquili (2001) have developed scientific models of meditation that show common brain changes through SPECT scans that occur during intensively religious moments. For example, a study of a group of Franciscan nuns at prayer revealed that at the exact moment such brain changes occurred, the sisters described it as the point where they experienced "a tangible closeness with God."

※ A psychological study found that Muslim patients who were depressed and received religious psychotherapy experienced a significantly quicker recovery than those depressed

Muslim patients who were treated by antidepressant medication in conjunction with standard supportive psychotherapy (Razali et al. 1998).

≪ In a study focusing on a group of adults with cancer, spirituality was found to be strongly associated with quality of life and satisfaction (Cotten et al. 1999).

We could go on and on with similar examples. Given this context, you can see why providing you with scientifically demonstrated effective means to enhance your well-being and improve your sense of self-worth, in concert with reaching your spiritual goals, is a potentially very powerful way to blend these two sets of healing forces.

For each journey, we will describe a set of life skills that will eventually help you to acquire an entire tool chest that can serve as a major resource for your journey. Using psychological tools in synchrony with one's spiritual belief systems is not a new idea. William James (1842-1910), who is often regarded as the father of American psychology, has been credited as being the first writer to use the term "self-esteem." However, he was also concerned with the "sick soul" and wrote extensively on the interplay between spirituality and health and well-being. James, a Harvard professor, described self-esteem as a self-feeling that depends upon what one decides to accomplish. He suggested that, although self-esteem can be raised by succeeding in our endeavors, it can also be raised through repeated disappointments. Centuries earlier, the Chinese sage Confucius said something quite similar: "Our greatest glory is not in never falling, but in rising every time we fall." As such, achieving our spiritual goals requires persistence and a change on our part that may involve a lowering or surrender of our pretensions—a change in our patterns of thinking and behavior to make them more consistent with our spiritual goals.

Changing these patterns can be very difficult. When such change is required, the insights and instruments available from psychological research can help. For example, many psychotherapy techniques employed by psychologists are designed to help people make changes in their thoughts, feelings, and behavior. As the strategies in this book are designed to boost personal efforts toward spiritual goals, it is likely that one's spiritual strengths will also boost the effects of the strategies. As such, rather than confine psychological interventions to a secular arena, this book will work to create a synergy—that is, a working and mutually enhancing relationship between spirituality and psychological science.

Getting Ready for the Journey

Note that we will not simply describe this journey. We think that you really do need to practice the tools provided along the way in order to have them work properly. There is an ancient Chinese proverb that we boxed to highlight its importance (note that we do this with other quotes throughout the book). Simply telling you what to do, according to this philosophy, would be ineffective. Rather, getting you involved—and we do hope you will get involved by learning and practicing the life skills—will help you to really "understand."

> **Tell me, I'll forget. Show me, I may remember. But involve me, and I'll understand.**
>
> **—Ancient Chinese proverb**

In becoming involved, we strongly suggest that after you read this introductory chapter, you go out and get a notebook or journal. There will be plenty of times throughout your journey that you will be asked to write things down. Research has found that writing ideas down increases the likelihood that you will remember the information as well as better understand it. Moreover, more recent studies have shown that "emotional writing," that is writing down your feelings about stressful events, serves to decrease negative physical and emotional consequences. Many people we have talked with prefer a journal, the kind that is often sold in bookstores. Others may prefer a simple notebook. In any case, it's important to have access to a journal or notebook while you're reading this volume because we will ask you to use it frequently.

While we're talking about getting prepared to go on your journey, you may wish to obtain an inexpensive tape recorder if you don't have one. Several of the tools in this book that involve relaxation instructions will be more effective if you don't have to try to relax while simultaneously trying to remember the instructions.

The Time to Pursue Your Spiritual Goals Is Now

For many reasons, the time for seeking such spiritual goals is the present. In a similar way to many other sudden tragedies and attacks throughout the world's history, the days following September 11, 2001 were marked by a collective yearning among people to refocus life on its "real meaning." Indeed, the desire to seek spiritual goals is often described as a basic human need.

A recent review of the scientific literature by a team of physicians at the prestigious Mayo Clinic (Mueller, Plevak, and Zummans 2001) suggested that, in general, research shows that:

« Most people have a spiritual life.

« Most patients want their spiritual needs assessed and addressed.

« Most studies have found a direct relationship between religious involvement and spirituality and better health outcomes.

« Supporting a patient's spirituality may enhance coping and recovery from illness.

As such, many people have begun spiritual journeys to increase their sense of peace, maximize mental and physical healing efforts, discover their life's purpose, and ultimately awaken one's self-esteem. Scientific studies have shown the results of such efforts. For example, recent studies of people who have experienced either sudden or gradual spiritual transformations indicate that they also experienced a change in how they viewed themselves—specifically, their sense of personal adequacy and competency was improved. In other words, their self-esteem may have been awakened. Whether through traditional world religions such as Buddhism, Christianity, Hinduism, Islam, Judaism, or more "new age" philosophies, increasing numbers of people are embarking on the challenging path of spiritual discovery. Even people who describe themselves as atheists or nonbelievers of a specific deity have embarked on similar goals with the objective of making their behavior and day-to-day existence more consistent with their moral values.

How Will You Use Your Future Moments?

How will you view each moment as it passes from the future to the past? If, while imagining the clock at the beginning of this chapter, you experienced any thoughts that were self-critical or judgmental, perhaps you will decide to make changes in your life so that you don't have to spend any more seconds, minutes, hours, or days hindered by self-doubt. If you're reading this book, it's likely that somewhere, deep down, you know that self-doubt, fear of your self-worth, and the continual need for approval from others, is a waste of your precious, passing lifetime. Instead, why not choose to spend this time on self-creation and self-acceptance? Now is the time to awaken the part of you that is lovingly connected with all other humans—your spirituality. Many people who have pursued their spiritual path have discovered that they can transform self-doubt into loving self-esteem. Such a transformation often involves a dramatic change in one's world view, one's sense of purpose, and changes in beliefs, attitudes, and behavior. We know that this sounds like a difficult and challenging journey. However, before you allow any negative thoughts to take hold concerning your own ability for this transformation, read on! We'll help you each step of the way. Take this spiritual journey with us. *Bon voyage!*

PART I

Spirituality and Self-Esteem: Preparing for the Journey

CHAPTER 1

Taking the First Steps

He who is outside the door has already
a part of his journey behind him.

—Dutch Proverb

The Challenge Ahead

Okay—you've decided to actually go on this journey. Now what?
You may be a bit worried about this trip you've committed to. The
problem with spiritual journeys is that they take a long time and
often occur over some pretty rough terrain. The word "journey" for
some can even conjure up an image of a very long trip—one that
requires lots of planning, involves meeting various challenges, and
includes many different stops along the way.

Given these concerns, this first chapter will provide tools to:

❦ Make the first steps in the journey a little easier,

❦ Help you to identify the barriers to reaching your spiritual
goals, and

❦ Help you to identify and prioritize the goals you wish to
work toward.

As this book is your travel guide for this personal journey, it has been organized to outfit you with effective tools to make traveling easier, more educational, and perhaps even fun at times! More importantly, it is our hope that the life tools we provide will help you reach the end of this journey—a place where you can awaken your self-esteem. So even if thinking about taking this journey appears somewhat scary right now, once you get these first tools in your grasp, you'll see your path open before you.

> **A journey of a thousand miles**
> **must begin with a single step.**
>
> **—Ancient Chinese proverb**

Your First Tool: Learning to Visualize

In this chapter, we will teach you to use visualization to help you to clarify your thinking about goals and to be better able to see the light at the end of the tunnel. Through such enhanced understanding, you can begin to get a better picture of your true desires and goals, not those that you feel you should have or ones that other people have imposed on you. Some have described this perspective as being able to know your "true self" or understanding your vital essence.

According to Zen teachings, an ultimate goal in cultivating wisdom is learning to see clearly exactly what one perceives, feels, and thinks as it is, without putting a layer of emotional filtering or intellectual interpretation on top of one's true experiences. Although visualization is not necessarily designed to help you to achieve "wisdom" as a Zen master would define it, it can be a great help in getting in touch with your true feelings, thoughts, and goals.

First we'll teach you how to use the visualization tool and then to apply it in a series of lessons geared to help you to eventually get in better touch with your true inner self, identify and prioritize those spiritual goals that are important to you, and develop an initial travel itinerary for your overall spiritual journey toward awakening self-esteem. Using visualization in these lessons will help substantially. The lessons include:

❦ Developing a visual picture of your future,

❊ Breaking down this picture into smaller steps,

❊ Identifying your unique barriers,

❊ Removing barriers to your goals,

❊ Translating barriers into thoughts, feelings, and actions to change,

❊ Charting your spiritual journey, and

❊ Prioritizing your spiritual goals.

What is Visualization?

Everyone can visualize. You visualize when you daydream, remember a past experience, picture a future vacation in your mind, or think of the people you know. Many psychologists and physicians believe that visualization can be a powerful tool to help us fulfill our dreams and achieve our life's goals. In sports, it's very common for athletes to use visualization to help their speed, strength, and performance. For example, skiers who visualize their downhill course and experience each turn with their eyes closed can actually improve their performance.

Visualization is the conscious and intentional creation of impressions that use all your five senses (that is, seeing, hearing, smelling, touching, tasting) for the purpose of changing yourself in some way. There are many different applications for visualization, as will be shown in future chapters. Learning this tool, then, is not only useful in helping to prepare for the journey at the beginning, but will be useful during other parts of your travels as well.

Getting Ready to Learn

Before you begin to use visualization to help you identify your spiritual goals, let's try learning some basics. In general, this tool helps you, in its most basic form, to create a multisensory image of various experiences in your mind's eye. To a large degree, these experiences will appear quite real because you're engaging all of your senses. For example, close your eyes for a few seconds now and imagine smelling your mother's kitchen, your morning coffee, the local bakery, or your favorite small bistro. We bet you can "smell" those wonderful aromas right now, even though you're not actually there.

To help you to learn this tool, try the following exercises. You can read them and try to visualize the images as best as possible, but we've found that if you tape record them, either in your own voice or having a family member or friend record them, it greatly enhances their effect. If you do record the instructions, read slowly and make sure to pause frequently in order to allow yourself sufficient time to create the images in your mind. It is usually a good idea to find a comfortable place in your home to practice this skill, ensuring a period of time when there are few interruptions.

❧ *General Visualization Script*

Let your eyes shut gently. Shut out the world, as you are about to start a voyage inward. Relax your muscles. Take a deep, slow breath.

Now, try to involve all of your senses. For example, try to visualize a piece of watermelon or other piece of fruit. Rather than just creating a visual picture in your mind, visualizing means hearing the crunch when you bite into it, feeling the cool, watery juice dripping onto your fingers and hands, smelling its unique scent, seeing the bright red color contrasted against the black, shiny seeds, and finally tasting the sweet meat of the watermelon itself.

You can practice using all your senses by trying some of these brief visualization exercises. To engage your sense of sight, imagine a black circle on a white background. Now change the color of the circle to red. Let the circle fade out until it becomes a dull pink. Now let it fade out entirely.

To engage your hearing, close your eyes and make all shapes and colors go away, imagining a gray dense fog. Now imagine you that hear a phone ringing. Let it ring five times, then stop. Now hear a siren or a car horn in the distance or a bird chirping overhead. Add some city sounds of construction, or a fire engine in the distance. Now hear a loved one say "I love you."

To engage your sense of touch, close your eyes and block out all visual or auditory images. Imagine sitting on a blanket with your toes in warm sand, or touching soft fur as you pet a cat, or feeling squishy suds in your hands.

Your sense of smell can be engaged by closing out all sights, sounds, and touch, and focusing on smelling fresh-baked bread, or salt air, or fresh cut grass, or coffee brewing in the next room.

Visualizing Your Safe Place

We have frequently taught people to visualize their "safe place" as a means to aid relaxation and general stress management. A safe place is where you can take a vacation in your mind, that is, feel relaxed, comfortable, and safe. For some, it may be a deserted island where only your spouse or significant other is with you, where the temperature is warm, but you can feel a soft breeze. You can hear the waves gently crashing on the sandy beaches and smell the salt air. For others, it may be a cozy cabin in the mountains, where the fireplace contains a warm, roaring fire, where you can smell the wood burning and hear the crickets outside. You get the picture!

This next exercise uses the visualization instructions to help you create your own safe place. We offer this exercise as a means of reducing any stress or tension that you might feel in general because it is a proven technique to reduce tension and anxiety. You can use the visualization in this manner at various times during your overall spiritual journey if you find yourself feeling stress, concerns, or worries. Using it will help to move you along just a little bit more toward your goals.

Once again, you can ask someone with a soft, soothing voice to read these instructions into a tape player so you have your own version. Remember, it's best to practice your visualization in a comfortable spot where you won't be interrupted. Try practicing this tool several times during this coming week, especially when you are not in a hurry and have the time to enjoy this "vacation."

⥤ *Safe Place Script*

Now you are going to go to your safe place. Take a nice, slow, deep breath. Now put your palms gently over your closed eyes and gently brush your hands over your eyes and face. Place your hands at your sides and allow your body to become relaxed all over. You are about to allow yourself to privately enter your own special place that is peaceful, comfortable, and safe.

You will fill your imagination of this place with rich detail. You will experience this place close up, looking off into the distance and using all of your senses. You can also allow room for another person such as your spouse, a friend, or a family member to be with you in this place if you choose.

Your safe place may be at the end of a boardwalk leading to a beach. Sand is under your feet, the water is about twenty yards away, and seagulls, boats, and clouds are in the distance. You feel the coolness of the air as a cloud passes in front of the sun and hear seagulls calling to each other. The sun is shimmering on the waves continually rolling to the shore, and there is a smell of salt from the boardwalk.

A different safe place might be a warm, wood-paneled den, with the smell of cinnamon buns baking in the oven down the hallway.

Through a window you can see fields of tall, dried corn stalks, and there is a crackling fire in the fireplace. A set of candles emit the aroma of lavender, and there is cup of tea on the table for you.

You may have a different safe place than these two scenes. Take a few seconds to identify your personal safe place. It can be the beach, a warm house, or anywhere else. The point is that it is your place to go to.

Keep your eyes closed and check your body for relaxation. Relax any muscles that still hold tension. Now walk slowly to your safe and quiet place. Let your mind take you there. Your place can be inside or outside, but wherever it is, it's peaceful and safe. Picture letting your anxieties and worries pass. Look to the distance . . . what do you see? Create a visual image of what you see in the distance. What do you smell? What do you hear? Notice what is right in front of you . . . reach out and touch it. How does it feel? Smell it . . . listen for any pleasant sounds. Make the temperature comfortable. Be safe here. Look around for a special, private spot. Feel the ground or earth under your feet . . . what does it feel like? Look above you. What do you see? What do you hear? What do you smell?

Now walk a bit farther and stop. Reach out and touch something lightly with your fingertips. What is the texture of what you are touching? This is your special place and nothing can harm or upset you here. You can come here and relax whenever you want. Stay in this safe and peaceful place for as long as you wish, allowing yourself to breath slowly and deeply and become relaxed all over.

Is there anyone else you wish to be with you? If so, imagine that they are now with you, also enjoying the peace and calm of your safe place. If not, that's fine—this is your vacation.

Now, slowly rise and leave your safe place by the same path or steps that you used to enter. Notice your surroundings. Say to yourself, "I can relax here. This is my special place, and I can come here whenever I wish."

Now slowly open your eyes and get used to your surroundings, but take with you the nice feelings of relaxation.

Visualizing to Identify Your Spiritual Goals

Now that you know how to use visualization, it's time to apply this tool to help better identify your spiritual goals as a means of getting closer to your true essence. When you think about what it takes to achieve goals, you will find that, to a large degree, it usually involves changing certain thoughts, feelings, or actions that stand in the way of achieving them. These may include self-doubts, negative feelings, or inadequate attempts to work towards your goals. By overcoming such negative influences, whether they come from you or from others, you will be better able to reach your objectives.

We'll guide you to use the visualization tool in order to gain a future vision of yourself as a means of determining what are those thoughts, feelings, and actions that currently may be blocking you from finding your vital essence. Right now, it may be difficult for you to see this part of yourself. In fact, learning to see the "real you" can be thought of as a major aim of this book in general, especially as it relates to helping you to awaken your self-esteem. Finding one's true or vital essence has been referred to in various spiritual philosophies as an activity that is central to major change, transformation, and even enlightenment. A major problem to achieve such knowledge is difficulty in overcoming barriers. Sometimes the barriers appear so overwhelming that it's difficult to see the real you. Consider the following true story of a child named Max.

Max's Story

When one of us (Christine) was working as a psychologist in an inner-city child psychiatry service several years ago, a three-year-old Latino child, Max, was referred for psychological evaluation. Max had been living on the city streets with a mother who had been recently hospitalized for drug addiction. To make matters worse, his father was in prison. Fortunately, Max had a paternal aunt who cared—he arrived at our clinic in her arms after she rescued him. At that time, he was covered in soil and skin sores, was dehydrated, and was wearing dirty diapers. Moreover, Max was functionally mute, unwilling or unable to speak to anyone. He appeared devoid of spirit, was uncommunicative, and behaved in a primitive manner. As an example, he had a tendency to bite and scream when approached.

> A rock pile ceases to be a rock pile the
> moment a single man contemplates it,
> bearing within him the image of a cathedral.
>
> —Antoine de Saint-Exupery

At first glance, the professionals in the clinic assumed that the child was deaf or mentally retarded and all agreed that it was difficult to assess him further until his emergent medical and dental needs received attention. After he did receive the necessary medical care, he returned to the child psychiatry service for assessment and treatment. What happened when all of the dirt, grime, hunger, dehydration, and harmful influences were removed was quite miraculous.

Supported by a very caring aunt who assumed the role of his foster mother, Max was found to be developmentally delayed, but only related to the neglect. In other words, there was no indication of chronic or nonreversible disability. By seeing past all of the barriers, his aunt worked with Christine in therapy for the next two years in order to give Max the best nurturance possible. This, fortunately, is a story with a happy ending. Max entered school by the age of five and at a developmental and adaptive level consistent with the other children his age. On the day that he was discharged from outpatient therapy, Max ran into the clinic jumping into Christine's arms, proud to show off pictures that he'd drawn for his class about his home, his new family, and his neighborhood. He was very eager to play "show and tell."

As you can imagine, this transformation was incredible to see. Two years prior, before all the barriers that blocked his progress could be removed, no one could have seen or understood the beauty that was Max. However, because his aunt believed in him and was unwilling to give up, with professional help, Max had a chance of actualizing his dreams.

What Are Your Barriers?

Although Max's situation was extreme, it serves as a useful metaphor to help prepare for visualizing your spiritual goals. Your ability to see yourself and your true essence or potential can be partially obscured by barriers that are difficult to see past. For example, the "dirt" and "hunger" that may be standing in your way may be your own past painful experiences or suffering, the lack of care you may have experienced from others, the negative things that you have learned to say to yourself, or the intense emotions you have tried to avoid. The following application of the visualization tool is designed to help create a glimpse of who you really are—your vital essence, the spiritual part of you waiting to be discovered.

Preparing for Visualization

In preparing to use this tool in this manner, it's important to choose a comfortable, relatively private place to engage in this visualization. Also, please have your journal ready to write down various things when requested to do so. In this section, we ask that you undergo several lessons, some of which involve using the visualization tool to increase your awareness. Follow these lessons, in a linear fashion, one by one. Move onto the next visualization lesson when you are ready. You can take anywhere from one day to several weeks to get through the next several lessons. If you decide to take some time with any one of the lessons, just make sure that you practice the visualization exercise that is described in that lesson at least once each day.

Lesson 1: Developing a Visual Picture of Your Future

Many times our personal goals are too vague and cloudy to really shoot for. For example, if your goal is to be kinder to others, what is the actual visual picture of this goal? Do you see yourself working at a homeless shelter? Are you shouting less and improving your communication with your children? Do you picture yourself seeing smiles in the faces of your customers? It's very important that you develop a visualization of the future in very specific and concrete mental pictures. Try it out right now. Describe the mental picture of what you want to change or accomplish and write down a description of that picture in your journal. For example, individuals who want to learn how to feel more fulfilled in their work or competent at their job may picture themselves in the company of their coworkers. They approach a person or a task that they may have found stressful or annoying in the past, but now have a feeling of comfort and inner peace. They picture themselves talking with the other person, speaking about their work with enthusiasm and confidence. They're not afraid that the other person will put down their ideas or sabotage their efforts. They are looking forward to some of the tasks they will be engaged in during the day as an opportunity to work through challenges that may occur.

If your mind starts to wander toward all the barriers or reasons why you can't change or accomplish what you want, *stop*. The purpose of this lesson is to simply allow yourself to imagine and describe a visual picture of your future self, as you see yourself progressing toward your spiritual goals. We will discuss barriers later. Go ahead—take a few moments to write down in your journal a concrete mental picture of what you want to change or accomplish. Don't try to include everything, just one thing. Use the heading "Lesson 1."

Lesson 2: Your Future in Steps

It's important to have both short- and long-term goals to visualize. For example, if a person's long-range goal is to manage anger more effectively, it would be very useful to create a series of images that may represent a series of steps to this goal. For example, a person may start with a short-range goal of reducing the time they shout at other people while driving. The image may be one of driving calmly and confidently down a busy street. A longer-range goal may be to reduce the anger they experience with their teenage child. The image here may be one of communicating effectively with their son or daughter. And so on. You will be much more successful in creating images or pictures of your spiritual goals by creating both long- *and* short-term goals in your visual images.

Remember to visualize goals in terms of things that can be accomplished. You can only make changes in yourself. For example, if your goal is to improve your relationship with your partner, goals such as "my partner will be more understanding" or "my partner will not drink so much" may not represent realistic goals because they are not in your control. They reflect the world as you want it to be, but not necessarily the way you can make it. However, goals such as "I will communicate my feelings or disagreements with my partner more effectively," "I will be more patient," or "I will no longer place myself in situations in which I am likely to be maltreated," are goals that can be achieved because they involve thoughts, feelings, or behavior that you can control. Remember that you can only change yourself—not others.

In addition, goals that are focused on changing the outcome of important external events (such as winning a contest or wanting someone's cancer to go away) will involve other factors that control the situation (as opposed to your own efforts). Your goals realistically need to be focused on what changes *you* can make that may help. With regard to the example of winning a contest, realistic goals may include performing your best or more effectively managing your anxiety concerning the event. With regard to facing the illness of a loved one with cancer, goals such as learning how to best provide caregiving duties, effectively helping in that person's recovery, or relieving suffering may serve as more realistic goals.

Right now, write down in your journal several short-term goals that would be useful to think of as "steps" toward the mental image you described earlier in Lesson 1. If you have difficulty immediately breaking down your vision of reaching spiritual goals or determining what are short- versus long-term objectives, don't worry. If you take a few moments to think about what steps would be involved in your original mental image of what you wish to accomplish, a few will come to mind. Write them down in your journal under the heading "Lesson 2." List both short-term *and* long-term steps.

Lesson 3: Removing the Barriers

In this lesson, you will use your imagination to travel to the future and visit yourself a few years from now. In this guided visualization, remember that all miracles are possible.

As with the previous visualization exercises, it's a good idea to make a tape-recording of the following script for yourself. If you work with a recorded script, it will be easier for you to play the tape and simply follow the instructions without putting pressure on yourself to remember the whole thing from your reading. Alternatively, you can have a friend or family member with a calming voice slowly read the script for you. In any event, the script should be read slowly, in a calm and quiet voice, with frequent pausing between sentences throughout. It should be listened to when you have at least twenty minutes to spare in which you can be by yourself in a quiet place with minimal interruption.

❧ *Removing Barriers Script*

Close your eyes and relax. Let go of all tension in your body. You are traveling to a safe and tranquil place in your mind, a special, outdoor place that you can go to in your imagination. You are here, in this imaginary place, right now. As you look around, take notice of what you see nearby, as well as in the distance. Describe the scene silently to yourself. Now look around for a path—this path is for you, and you are starting on it right now, walking slowly toward the future to your home. Notice a tree stump or log branch across the path. Imagine that this piece of wood is getting in the way of your ability to continue down the path. This piece of wood is your hesitation, your fear of changing, or your fear of working toward your goals. As you step over the branch, you are overcoming your hesitation to start your spiritual journey—you are actually moving a fear aside.

Now, as you walk along the path, you come to a steep hill. This hill is made up of the doubts that you have about yourself. Start up the hill and keep walking even though you're not certain what you will find at the top. With each step, however, you are beginning to feel more confident that you're getting closer to reaching your spiritual goals. Feel the anxiety and worries slip away.

When you are close to the top, you must walk through a dark and murky forest in which the trees are blocking out the sunlight. This forest is dark, cold, wet, and muddy. It has all the obstacles that block you from seeing your final goals—the interference and criticism from others, day-to-day problems, a desire to right all the wrongs done to you, your need for approval from others, and your own fears that you don't deserve to have such inner peace. As you walk on, you walk a little more slowly, weighed down by the heavy wet mud on your feet, and even though you have come this far, it is difficult to continue— but you do. You feel a renewed strength, knowing that all you need to do is put one foot in front of another, one by one. You are committed to continuing your journey.

Somehow, you are able to tolerate your fear and any other negative feeling that you experience as you trudge through this dark forest. Note how good this feels. You push past the trees, come out onto a clearing, and are now in the open and can see and feel the sun's warmth. This could be a lovely meadow or field, a beautiful beach with sand dunes, or a mountaintop. Take a few moments to picture this safe and peaceful place in your mind's eye. You can see your home. This is your true home even though you may have actually just arrived for the first time, a place where you know that you're meant to be. You know this because as soon as you walk through the door, you are overwhelmed with a sense of light, love, peace, and fulfillment.

You know you're home because you have caught a glimpse of this feeling before—just briefly. It may have been for just a moment as you heard a child laugh, or heard a compelling sequence of music, or watched a wave crash against a rock. It reminds you of looking up at night into a very clear sky, seeing the millions of bright stars, feeling very much a part of the universe.

As you walk into your home, this feeling is predominant, rather than fleeting. As you enter your home, what do you see?

Follow yourself through one day. What gives you enjoyment? As you picture yourself here, in the future, imagine what you are doing at work, or what you are learning. Now look back a bit and picture the life experiences that brought you the greatest joy and sense of purpose. Maybe you ran a marathon, taught a neighbor to read, baked a cake for someone confined to their home by illness, gave a great speech, helped a friend to change a tire, watched the ocean, cooked a good meal, held a child, sang or prayed during a religious service, cried when you were moved by a sad movie, or many other things.

Try to actually visualize yourself at home. When you have finished exploring, let your images fade away and come back to the present, the here and now. Open your eyes and take a deep breath.

Lesson 4: Identifying Your Personal Barriers

Hopefully, you have been able to "see the future." While the images are still fresh in your mind, make a brief list of your own personal barriers. These are the "rocks" and "tree branches" that you had to step over, the hills of doubt you had to climb, the obstacles that you visualized as standing in the way of being the person that you saw in your visualization. For example, you may have the image of your ideal future as feeling relaxed, loved, experiencing the joys of seeing family or friends, or looking back on a day in which you accomplished something worthwhile. If so, then one possible barrier to achieving such a future may be feelings of jealously or resentment you have toward others—always feeling that other people have it better than you. Working toward the spiritual goal of acceptance may remove some of these barriers. If so, this may be a goal that you should prioritize.

On the other hand, you may have visualized a future where you have close relationships with many people, enjoying their company and their wisdom. Perhaps a barrier for you is the difficulty you have letting go of anger when you perceive people treating you with disrespect—those people who cut you off in traffic or talked loudly during the movies or didn't give you the raise you think you deserve. If so, an important spiritual goal for you, then, might be working towards being able to forgive people more readily.

Go ahead and write down the barriers you see in yourself. These are the barriers that you imagined as represented by the logs in the road, the hill, and the dark and murky forest in the visualization script. Write these barriers in your journal under the heading, "My Barriers."

Lesson 5: Translating Barriers

Identifying these barriers may be somewhat distressing. Right now, you may be feeling somewhat overwhelmed, not knowing how to overcome these barriers. However, the strength of these obstacles can be lightened through work toward your spiritual goals using the tools in this book. To help continue to motivate you, we offer another inspirational saying, this one by William Ward: "Adversity causes some men to break, others to break records." Given this, you might be asking, "How can I break records? How can I accomplish my goals?"

The very next step at this point is to translate these barriers in a way that identifies specific ways to overcome them using the tools provided in this book. In other words, by defining your barriers in terms of negative thoughts, feelings, and actions that can be changed, you can more easily search for ways to modify them. Not coincidentally, the tools offered in this book can help you change three types of barriers: negative thoughts, feelings, and actions that serve as obstacles in attaining emotional and spiritual growth.

Thoughts

Thoughts, also referred to as cognitions, are the statements that you make silently to yourself. Sometimes these thoughts appear loud and clear in your mind, allowing you to be consciously aware of them. At other times, your thoughts may occur automatically, as an image or brief remembrance of a past event, for instance. When this happens, your thoughts occur so quickly that they seem to be just below the line of your conscious radar.

Because they occur so quickly and you are not completely aware they are happening, they often are instantly or automatically perceived as accurate. Such automatic thoughts are instantly believed to be true by the person experiencing them. This is an important point, because the automatic thoughts may be true—or *they may be false*. They may provide a commentary that is accurate. For example, when observing a coworker of yours receiving praise from a supervisor, you might say to yourself, "Bob looks happy to receive such praise." Conversely, your thoughts may reflect certain assumptions that are not accurate at all, but reflect how you have learned to think about such situations. For example, when observing the same scene, you may say to yourself, "Bob always gets noticed—he always gets all the breaks," or "I'll never get the kind of praise that Bob gets." As you can imagine, such different thoughts are likely to result in very different feelings. In the first instance, you are observing a fact, that Bob seems happy. However, in the second series of thoughts, you're likely to experience some negative feelings in the form of envy and jealousy as you compares yourself to Bob and assume a negative and hopeless outcome for yourself.

Many people who experience anxiety and depression have thinking styles in which a negative type of thinking appears to maintain a cycle of sad or worried feelings. Therapists that specialize in a form of psychotherapy called cognitive therapy have developed very useful strategies for people to learn in order to change their negative and inaccurate thoughts to more accurate thinking and to rely less on assumptions. We will talk more about this in chapter 4.

Assumptions which occur automatically can be troublesome when they consist of thoughts that distort the facts or reality in some way, yet occur so quickly and frequently that we accept them as true. Are some of the obstacles getting in the way of your spiritual goals due to the thoughts that occur automatically in your head? Do you find yourself worried about what other people might think? This often means that *you are the one who is actually thinking this way and criticizing yourself.* Many of the tools in this book contain techniques that have been developed through decades of clinical research to help people make the kinds of changes in their thinking styles that are needed for spiritual growth. Through such strategies, people have learned that they can control their mind, rather than allow their mind to control them.

Write down a few examples of the types of thoughts that you would like to experience as part of your spiritual journey. Write them down under the heading "Thoughts" in your journal. These may include having more positive thoughts about yourself or others or experiencing fewer critical or angry thoughts.

Feelings

Feelings reflect our subjective experiences from moment to moment and can include a wide range and type of emotions. Sadness, awe, fear, anger, joy, and exhilaration are all examples of the changing feelings we experience throughout our life. Note that emotions can occur simultaneously, even if they seem to be in conflict with one another. For example, people have described the phenomena during a funeral of being both sad for the loss of a loved one but also happy and amazed regarding how the person lived their life.

Emotions often result from the thoughts that we experience. For example, after thinking that we regret something we've done or worrying that we won't be able to do something in the future, we may feel sad or fearful.

Feelings also involve physiological changes. As human beings, our minds and bodies have adapted over many years to react to instances of danger. For example, when we experience any form of threat, our bodies are instantly triggered into action by the most primitive parts of our brain. This part of the brain is constantly tuned into any possible threat from the environment, and it is the reason why you can be awakened from a sound sleep by even a very mild noise or why you experience a surge of physiological change when startled. Your heart beats faster, your blood is pumped to your muscles, you begin breathing rapidly, and you undergo a series of neuroendocrine changes (that is, changes in the way your brain and hormonal system communicate) that help to prepare your body to either stand and fight or run away. You are most keenly aware of the phenomena when you're frightened, jealous, or angry. However, when this type of reaction occurs with significant frequency, you may ultimately experience feeling sad, tired, in pain, or even emotionally numb.

Because feelings are not only inevitable, but in their basic design can be quite useful and adaptive, some of the tools in this book are designed to help you manage these feelings and use them effectively when they occur. This involves practicing ways to accept your feelings, to better understand what your body is telling you, and to learn to break any cycles in which you are negatively interpreting your feelings. If you are experiencing difficulty with feelings, we hope that the tools in this book will help you to see them as part of the valuable equipment you need on your spiritual journey. This is probably a very different view than you might have of negative emotions, but one that is extremely important to adopt in order to experience meaningful change.

Right now, write down the feelings that you want to manage more effectively or those that you would like to experience more often. Write them down in your journal under the heading "Feelings."

Actions

Actions involve things we do or have done. Also referred to as our overt behavior, actions, in contrast to thoughts and emotions, are phenomena that other people observe or that we observe in ourselves. For example, giving a great speech or shouting at a family member during a holiday dinner are instances of more public actions. Cheating on your income tax, spreading a rumor, or singing in the shower are examples of actions that are more private and individually experienced.

One aspect of actions or behavior about which most therapists agree is that behavior that has occurred in the past tends to repeat itself. This is because our actions are ongoing products of both our inherited characteristics and the learning environments we have experienced throughout our lives. Thus, we have learned to respond to our own internal thoughts and feelings, as well as the actions of others, in very characteristic ways. These behavior patterns are often reflected in the way we either describe ourselves or the ways in which other people describe us. For example, descriptions such as, "Jim always thinks he's right," "Jenny really knows how to roll up her sleeves and work hard," or "Bart is a good listener, " all may reflect behavior patterns that other people have observed about Jim, Jenny, or Bart. Behavior that you observe about yourself, such as "I am socially skilled," "I'm a klutz when it comes tennis," or "I can't carry a tune," are examples of self-assessments that are made after observing your actions.

Actions that we view either positively or negatively can also be infrequent or reoccurring behaviors. For example, you may positively view your ability to sing each week in church (a frequent behavior), or you may remember the one time you rescued a wounded animal (an infrequent behavior) as important positive actions. Conversely, you may view your frequent angry outbursts while driving with an equal degree of regret as the one time you forgot to attend your child's soccer match.

Many of the tools in this book are designed to help you change your patterns of behavior and actions. This involves practicing ways of doing something different than your current behavior patterns that interrupt or block your spiritual journey. You are probably saying to yourself right now that this is very difficult to do. That's why we provide the specific tools for behavior change in this book as well.

Take a few moments to write down which behaviors or actions you would like to identify as part of the change process associated with your spiritual journey. These may include taking more risks, wasting less time, or doing more for others. Go ahead and write these down in your journal under the heading "Actions."

Lesson 6: Charting Your Spiritual Journey

Okay, now you have a lists of thoughts, feelings, and actions that you would like to change in yourself. Now choose at least *three* of these thoughts, feelings, or actions. Picking three things to change makes it seem easier and less overwhelming. It also helps you to prioritize what is most important to you. You may choose three thoughts, feelings, or actions—or choose one each—whatever is most important to you. This new list could be changes that you want to make within yourself or changes regarding your relationship with others. Feel free to write down more if you like, but list at least three. These may be stated as things you would like to experience more (like "feeling relaxed"), as well as to experience less (such as feeling angry).

Below is an example of the thoughts, feelings, and behaviors that one of our clients, Eve, developed. Eve was a thirty-seven-year-old mother of two children who found herself "burning the candle at both ends." A working single mother, Eve's days were spent trying to complete her work as a college administrator, running to her children's various activities after school or helping with their homework, and often engaging in ongoing arguments with her former spouse over issues of child support and visitation. In her visualization of the future, she pictured herself as feeling confident in her accomplishments, having quality time to spend with her children, and imagined a less hectic lifestyle. Eve saw herself as calmer, more patient in her negotiations with her children's father (described by Eve as "not letting him push my buttons"), and relating better to her own family members and friends.

Below is an example of her list of thoughts, feelings, and actions that she wanted to change.

Eve's List

❦ Changes in thoughts: Have more thoughts of self-confidence; stop worrying about getting others' approval

❦ Changes in feelings: Stop feeling angry or resentful because of what other people have; feel more comfortable when I am alone

❦ Changes in actions: Doing more of what I choose to do rather than what others expect; calm down and not let my former husband "get to me"

Now use Eve's list as an example to help you make up your own. Are there any similarities? Any differences?

Lesson 7: Prioritizing Your List

After you have constructed your own list, take a few moments to prioritize the items. Recalling the visualization of you in your "true home," unencumbered by fears and doubts and discovering your true essence, list the changes that you would like to make in order of importance (most important first). List these in the form of goals. As an example, here is Eve's list after she thought about what she wanted to do first. Parenthetically, in making this new priority list, she started to feel nervous and experience self-doubt. However, having previously learned to use visualization as a relaxation tool, she went to her safe place, felt physically calmer, and started to think about some of the quotes we had previously given her—the quotes, for example, included in this chapter. As a consequence, she was able to make this new list.

Here is Eve's new priority list of goals:

1. Stop worrying about getting other's approval.

2. Calm down and not let my former husband get to me.

3. Have more thoughts of self-confidence.

4. Do more of what I choose to do rather than what others expect of me.

5. Stop feeling angry because other people are smarter, richer, or more confident.

6. Feel more comfortable when I am alone.

Go ahead now and make your own priority list of goals.

Table 1. Spiritual Goals and Tools for Your Journey

Chapter 3: Enhancing Relationships

Changing Thoughts: Changing negative thinking

Changing Feelings: Developing empathy and compassion skills

Changing Behavior: Getting support you need from others

Chapter 4: Fostering Acceptance

Changing Thoughts: Changing the myths about feeling good
Accepting negative events, change, and loss

Changing Feelings: Fostering gratitude

Changing Behavior: Making mistakes

Chapter 5: Learning to Forgive

Changing Thoughts: Challenging unforgiving thoughts
Adopting the 30 percent solution
Learning that enemies are teachers in disguise

Changing Feelings: Leaving the battlefield
Using visualization
Quieting down your angry body
Autogenic training

Changing Behavior: Learning to really listen
Carrying out your forgiveness plans

Chapter 6: Increasing Patience

Changing Thoughts: Seeking help from your Higher Power

Developing Your Travel Itinerary

Now that you have this list of prioritized goals, look at table 1 and read over the various spiritual goals that will be addressed in future chapters. These particular goals are included because they're the goals that we have most frequently heard people identify as important to work towards over the past twenty-plus years of our practice. In addition, these types of goals are frequently identified as significant among many spiritual philosophies and religions.

Looking at your *two* goals of highest priority. Where do they fit with regard to the various spiritual goals that are addressed in the other book chapters? For example, Eve's top two goals were to stop worrying about getting other people's approval and to calm down and not allow her former husband "get to her," that is, to not get so angry when speaking with him. These goals seemed to suggest that a good place for her to start her journey was with the chapters entitled "Fostering Acceptance" (chapter 4) and "Learning to Forgive" (chapter 5). Her focus on winning everyone's approval had given her some short-term feelings of being loved, but Eve knew deep down that she wanted to discover what was important to her, and not always be worried about others' needs exclusively. She also experienced the anger that she harbored toward her former husband as very distressful. Although she wanted to forgive him and communicate differently for the children's sake, she found it too difficult to carry through. Therefore, these two spiritual goals appeared very meaningful for her to prioritize.

Note that in the table, the tools that will be described in each chapter, along with instructions for how to use or practice each tool, are listed according to their focus on changing thoughts, feelings, or behaviors. As we mentioned earlier, this book does not have to be read from cover to cover (although you certainly can choose to read it in this manner). Rather, it's designed for you to travel your journey according to your own route (in this case, choice of chapter sequence), taking as long as you like to stop and visit along the way. Would reading the whole book in sequence be the most beneficial? Sure—that's why we wrote it this way. But again, there may be goals that you prioritized that are covered in chapters further along in the book. Don't hesitate to go to them first. However, before you start your unique journey, please read the next chapter, called "Awakening Spiritual Awareness." We believe this chapter is vital to help you make the most out of the journey—regardless of your specific travel itinerary.

The Journey Itself Is Significant

In a way, the end of this journey is actually a new beginning. Although awakening self-esteem is the ultimate destination, the tools that are provided to help reach each specific spiritual goal along the way will provide you with a set of tools to use as you continue along your path to reach any new emotional or spiritual destination. Recall the last time you took a long trip. It would be very unusual to hear anyone say that the trip was made with only the final end in mind. In fact, most people would indicate that the planning, anticipation, and discoveries made along the way actually added to the excitement and joy of travel. When you embark on a spiritual journey, it is much the same. A spiritual journey is also a lifelong process (some spiritual traditions suggest that it is a "many lives" process). As such, it is the discoveries along the way and the anticipation of the next experience that often motivates us as travelers to go on. In this context, here's another quote to think about, this one from Ursula Le Guin, "It is good to have an end to journey toward, but it is the journey that matters in the end."

CHAPTER 2

Enhancing Your
Spiritual Awareness

Know ye not ... that the spirit of God dwelleth within you?

—I Corinthians 3:16

Why Increase Your Spiritual Awareness?

At this point, not only have you decided to attempt this spiritual journey, but you've probably already developed a travel plan or itinerary. Perhaps, based on the lessons completed in chapter 1, you identified two or three chapters that you want to go to immediately after reading this chapter. Or, perhaps you decided to read each chapter in sequence in order to maximize the number of life skills that you can learn, as well as to increase your chances of attaining the final destination of awakening your self-esteem. In any case, we asked that you read this chapter on spiritual awareness prior to embarking on your journey to any of the various destinations. Why? Because we want you to be "awake" to appreciate and get the most out of the journey.

Recall past trips or journeys that you took. Being awake helped you to see all the sights you wanted to, to appreciate the landscape that you crossed getting from one destination to another, to better plan for side trips, to enjoy the good weather that you were fortunate to have, and to notice the smaller things that caught your eye when you were looking. In a similar vein, being more spiritually awake allows you to obtain a fuller, richer, and more enjoyable overall experience on your pending journey, as well as in life in general.

Waking Up

In most spiritual belief systems, there are many references to the awe-inspiring beauty to be discovered in the existence of life itself with all its imperfections and uncertainties. This awareness has inspired prophets, priests, writers, philosophers, artists, healers, sages, and mystics since the dawn of time. For people who are spiritually aware, regardless of their specific faith or belief system, miracles and insights can often be found in seemingly mundane moments, encounters, activities, or day-to-day events.

This chapter will provide you with tools and specific strategies that can help you enhance your spiritual awareness. For example, based on certain Eastern philosophies and faiths, meditative exercises have been developed around activities such as sitting, walking, or eating. While practicing an eating meditation, for example, a small morsel of food, such as a piece of bread, a grape, or a morsel of rice is first carefully observed and then appreciated. The piece of food is experienced using all the senses, examined for texture, aroma, physical appearance, and even sound, as it may be held up to the ear. There is an awareness and gratitude for having the food—especially in light of the problems of hunger and poverty present in our world. When the food is finally tasted, it is slowly moved over the insides of the mouth, noted, and savored.

As one engages in such a meditative experience of a simple activity that they have done thousands of times before, a realization can emerge of how we have all learned to go through our day without really being aware of such a potentially pleasant experience. This is similar to disregarding a precious gift. Have you ever eaten food without even tasting it because you were so hungry that you just shoveled it in? Such is a waste of a pleasurable event!

This simple activity can serve as a very useful metaphor for our other life experiences. For instance, we are often in the physical presence of another person, but our mind gets preoccupied, preventing us from connecting with this person. We wake up and go about our tasks and work, unaware of all of our mind's activities that have obscured what is truly important to our spiritual growth. There are often positive experiences that we're missing at any moment, as well as negative emotional experiences that can help us to better understand how we have learned to ignore our incredible worth and value as human beings. If we are not awake, we can literally miss thousands and thousands of valuable experiences that can enrich our lives and even foster our spiritual growth.

The Advantages of Awareness

When people are aware of their true essence, their vision is less hindered with regard to setting personal goals for change, being motivated to put their values into practice, and solving day-to-day problems. Techniques that are designed to remove the barriers of a busy mind can be powerful tools in and of themselves to decrease anxiety and to increase a sense of well-being and calmness. Moreover, the techniques that help us to observe our often self-destructive "mind habits" can also facilitate spiritual awareness and serve as important precursors to practicing many of the tools we provide to help you reach the other spiritual goals in this book.

> **There is nothing more wonderful than the soul of man.**
>
> **—Hazrat Inayat Kahn**

In this chapter, we provide specific strategies to help foster your spiritual awareness. The first tool, called *mindfulness meditation,* involves learning how to stay in the present moment—becoming more aware of your surroundings as well as your internal experiences without judgment or evaluation. This tool can also help you to be more appreciative of the transient nature of reality and to accept change as inevitable.

A Zen Moment

We remember our first exposure to Buddhist philosophy several years ago and becoming perplexed when reading the many descriptions of Zen teaching in which a master would answer a student's request for an explanation of a concept through a seemingly unrelated action—like a whack with a stick or a knock on the head. Of course we thought, "What the heck is going on here?" However, we came to believe that in the context of learning to master an understanding of the importance of the moment, such behavior may actually be quite educational. At least occasionally, this type of practice may indicate that if one is not carried away by their thoughts and can remain alert to the moment, they may have seen the whack coming and been able to avoid it. By learning to stay in the present, we are able to better observe the frequent mind games, or negative thoughts and emotions we experience and target them for change. Such skills can greatly increase our personal wisdom and ultimately help to awaken our self-esteem. This philosophy is nicely illustrated in the following quote provided by Ramaswami and Sheikh (1989, p. 91) who describe the perspective of Gautama Siddhartha, who after his own enlightenment and transformation process, became known as the Buddha.

> Such was the Buddha's impact that people sometimes felt he must be something more than human. "Are you a God? " they asked. "No." "Are you an angel?" No." "A saint?" "No." "Then what are you?" they asked. "I am awake," replied the Buddha.

In the next section, we describe mindfulness meditation, a tool that you can use to increase your own spiritual awareness and become more mindful of your day-to-day experience.

Mindfulness Breathing Meditation

"Mindfulness" refers to a meditative practice that has been an integral part of spiritual training for centuries in various Eastern faiths, such as Buddhism. It has been described as a state of nonjudgmental awareness—essentially, the ability, through practice, to be fully aware of a situation without having to add anything to it and without judging what you're experiencing. Similar in practice to the relaxation tools developed by behavioral psychologists and physicians, practicing mindfulness is important because it allows us to more fully experience what is happening in the present moment (that is, our breathing, our bodily sensations, our immediate environment, our movement, our present activity).

What is Mindfulness Meditation?

The term mindfulness generally refers to the state of consciousness wherein a person is highly aware and focused on the reality of the present moment—where they are able to both accept and acknowledge this present reality without getting caught up in thoughts about the situation or their emotional reaction to the situation. According to Goldstein and Kornfield, two leading meditation teachers, "It has a quality of fullness and impeccability to it, a bringing of our whole heart and mind, our full attention, to each moment" (Marlatt and Kristeller 1999, p. 62).

Mindfulness mediation is a method that can be applied to coping with stressful events such that a person approaches such situations "mindfully" in order to respond to them rather than automatically reacting to them in ways that may have been maladaptive or destructive in the past. Research continues to find this approach to be very effective for a variety of anxiety and stress disorders. Alan Marlatt, a behavioral psychologist, has found this approach to be helpful in the treatment of various addictions, such as excessive drinking and alcoholism. In addition, Dr. Jon Kabat-Zinn, a pioneer in the application of this approach in medicine, has repeatedly found mindfulness meditation to be effective in reducing chronic pain (Kabat-Zinn 1995).

An important goal of mindfulness mediation is to be able to distance oneself from one's experiences creating a sort of persona of separateness. This "independent" observer or onlooker pays close attention to one's thoughts and feelings as they occur in the present moment, but the person attempts to separate such thoughts and feeling from their trueessence. In other words, we can eventually, through this process, come to truly understand that *we are not our thoughts* and *we are not our feelings.* In this way, we can observe (what might be negative) thoughts and feelings as we experience them, but realize that we don't have to allow these thoughts and feelings to force us to act in a certain way. As such, the thought of "I feel so stupid today for forgetting my planning book at home" is just a thought! We can note it, observe it, and even see it pass by. But most importantly, we don't have to *react* to such a thought as if it's the universal truth and then feel bad about ourselves. We can simply acknowledge, with detached acceptance, that we had the thought. The thought doesn't own us, nor does it define us—it's just a thought.

We have found that the metaphor of looking at movies of yourself or hearing tape-recordings of your voice can be a useful way to help you to be a detached observer. Seeing a movie of yourself allows you to see yourself outside of your own body, as it were. You're actually seeing yourself say and do things—but it really isn't you. If you can refrain from evaluating these actions, but rather simply note that you are engaged in them, then you can begin to see your thoughts and feelings from a distance. If you have ever taken any home movies, go look at them now and try to simply observe yourself. Try to observe yourself without any judgments, being more accepting and forgiving of any actions you previously would have felt embarrassed by (or even proud of). Simply observe—don't judge.

Going Out of Your Mind

Please note that this heading doesn't imply that we want you to go crazy or that this tool will lead to any loss of control. Instead, it refers to a way of releasing you from your mind's tendency to fill up with thoughts of guilt, resentment of the past, or preoccupation with the future. Any of these types of thoughts can only take you away from experiencing the present moment. More importantly, by focusing on the present moment, you can get in better touch with your true essence.

Take the next few minutes to try this brief experiment. Close your eyes, clear your mind, and just observe the first thought of which you are conscious. You may actually be thinking, "What *is* the first thought that comes into my mind?" It may take a few seconds or several minutes. What was the thought? It may have been a comment on the exercise, such as "This seems silly," "I wonder if I'm doing this right?" or "I can't take time to do this now—I'm wasting time!"

We hope that the outcome of this exercise will help to underscore several important points about how to practice mindfulness meditation. These include:

* As long as you are in a state of intense presence, you're free of thought—you are still, your mind is calm, yet you remain highly alert.

* The instant your conscious attention slips a bit, a thought rushes in that takes you away from the moment.

* The brief time that you had a clear mind, as well as the time you were observing a thought that popped into your head, you were in the moment, aware of your thought, waiting for it, and able to notice it without evaluation, accepting whatever was there. This, essentially, is the definition of mindfulness.

* The thought you experienced probably contained some kind of critique, worry, instruction, memory, daydream, positive or negative judgment about yourself. This is how your mind has generally learned to pull you away from the moment.

❧ If you're able to observe your mind "speaking" or transmitting a thought, remember that *you are not your mind*. Your mind is essentially a tool that can be used to help connect you with your true essence. Alternatively, it can also work against you and lead you to chronically avoid or ignore the precious (and many would say sacred) experience that is your life. By learning to separate and disengage your mind's thinking habits from who you are, you'll become more aware of your own purpose and possibilities, as well as the beauty that exists in the world.

Unlearning Old Thinking Habits

The mindfulness meditation tool is designed to help you develop your mindfulness skills. We need to practice these skills because it takes effort to undo or "unlearn" the habit of ignoring our inner energies and allowing our minds to trigger negative emotions. When this negativity occurs, it can set us on a potentially destructive path of behavior. Over the years, you have learned to automatically respond to your mind telling you that you must gain approval from others, avoid unpleasant thoughts, feelings, or memories, and ignore who you really are. Paradoxically, the reason for this actually involves the way in which the brain works. Human beings have a uniquely sophisticated way of processing information through words that allows the capability for great insights and innovations. However, at the same time, this very complex type of information processing helps us avoid danger in order to survive. This can be very useful when you're confronted with a physically dangerous situation, in which your mind will use all of its processing abilities to put information together to warn you of the danger.

This same ability, however, can be useless and destructive when it puts information together to warn you of *nondeadly* consequences. Day-to-day examples of the mind warning you of this type of "danger" include embarrassment, fear of the unknown, confusion, hostility, and a need for approval. In other words, your mind will often automatically react to things like humiliation, minor conflict, or the unfamiliar as though they were life threatening. Responding to such thinking habits can take you away from being present in a meaningful life moment. Meditation is practiced to connect you with your inner energies or life force and to stop shutting yourself off from your potential. Ultimately, by setting your goals to focus more on the here and now, you can realign yourself with your true path—the path to self-awareness and enhanced self-esteem.

Now let's learn how to meditate in a mindful manner. The best time to practice this meditation tool may be in the early morning, just after awakening. That's when you have had some rest and haven't yet turned on the television or radio to begin the bombardment of messages to your mind. You can choose any place to engage in mindfulness breathing—your office, before retiring for the night, in your car while waiting to pick up your children, or even while waiting for a red light to change.

You may practice this meditation with your eyes open or closed. Some people find it easier to tune into their breathing when their eyes are closed. However, this would not be advisable in certain situations, such as when you're driving or sitting in traffic. Initially, set aside about ten minutes to engage in this mindfulness breathing meditation exercise. You can extend the time after you've practiced a bit. Similar to the visualization exercises you learned in chapter 1, you may wish to tape record the following instructions in order to free you from having to remember them.

1. Begin by feeling your breath. Do not *think* about it, just feel it come in.

2. Notice how it stops, it reverses, then it flows out.

3. There is no special way to breathe. Any way you breathe is natural. It is your life force.

4. Think of your breath as being like a rising wave—it happens on its own. Just stay with that image and be mindful of the breath in your body.

5. Your mind is not going to want to stay on the breath for very long. When that happens and you drop your focus on your breathing, just let the mind go off—but let it also come back.

6. Keep your body loose and still.

7. Feel the breath.

8. Breathe in . . . breathe out

9. As you breathe in, focus on the breath. Think, "I am accepting life."

10. As you exhale, focus on the breath. Think, "I am giving life.

11. Ride the breath.

12. Flow with the breath.

13. Feel it in your nostrils.

14. Feel your abdomen rise and fall (place your hands on your stomach area if you prefer to feel the flow of your breath).

15. Rest your mind on the simple, regular, calming wave of breathing that your body is experiencing.

16. Notice the sensation in your nostrils, abdomen, and shoulders.

17. Notice any thoughts that bubble up to the surface of your mind. Notice them and simply let them go. Remember that these thoughts are not you. You are not defined by your thoughts.

18. Settle in the present moment. Stay aware of actual moment-to-moment happenings—a slight pain in your shoulder or various sounds, such as a train passing by, the wind rustling through the trees, or people's voices.

19. Let your concentration deepen.

20. Don't try to suppress your perceptions, feelings, or aware-ness—simply notice what is happening and then let it dis-solve as the new moment begins.

21. Stay awake, even if your eyes are closed. Remain alert . . . pay attention.

22. Breathe in . . . breathe out. Stay focused.

23. Let go of each breath. Let go of each thought—don't hang on.

24. Note your thoughts. Notice them and let them go. With each breath, let go of any thoughts a little bit more. Let them simply pass by.

25. Notice where your mind is when it's not on your breathing.

26. Make no judgment, just notice where it is and come back to the breath

27. Allow each moment to be fresh and new.

After engaging in several practice sessions, it's likely that you will have experienced several moments in which you were able to let the noise of your mind fade in the background and you can experi-ence the present moment. Try to practice this tool at least once a day for a week or two. We suggest that you consider practicing this tool once a week for the rest of your life.

After each session, write down any impressions you have in your journal—whether you enjoyed the meditation or any ideas on how you can enhance your own ability to be in the moment. Such thoughts and feelings over time can provide meaningful insight concerning your overall journey. In the next section, we will teach you another tool, this one more action oriented. We'll be taking a "wabi-sabi walk." This walk is designed to help extend the experience of mindfulness for you and works very nicely with the mindfulness meditation tool you just learned.

Taking A Wabi-Sabi Walk

Wabi-sabi is a term used to describe a Japanese philosophical and artistic concept that is somewhat difficult to translate into English, but essentially consists of a way of perceiving your surroundings in a certain way. In other words, it represents a particular type of world view. Within this world view, there is recognition of the beauty in things that are imperfect, impermanent, or incomplete. You can imagine that if everyone in the world believed in a wabi-sabi perspective, there would be a predictable increase in self-acceptance and self-esteem.

> **All truths are easy to understand once they are discovered; the point is to discover them.**
>
> **—Galileo**

The concept of wabi-sabi also involves observing the beauty in things modest and humble, as well as unconventional. Several years ago, while touring the Holocaust Museum in Washington DC, we attended a special exhibition that described the exodus of a community of Eastern European Jewish refugees who had escaped the Nazi regime. For many reasons of politics, chance, and the particular people involved in their escape, this group of refugees ended up for some time in Japan. The description of the refugees' acceptance by their host community was striking, as the Japanese people must have viewed foreigners as "impermanent," "unconventional," and "incomplete." Perhaps the characteristic wabi-sabi perspective facilitated their view of the beauty that was to be found in these strangers who neither spoke their language nor engaged in their customs, indeed, appearing very different. This exhibition left us with a hopeful understanding that one's view of the world can be marked by the recognition of a universal human connection, rather than characterized by a strong fear of differences.

A Spiritual Tradition

The concepts of wabi-sabi fit well with other concepts described in the teachings of Zen Buddhism. This is not surprising in that the first Japanese people involved in wabi-sabi were tea masters and Zen priests. Although the route of Buddhism originated in India, then onto China, and only eventually reached Japan in the twelfth century, it was the Zen Buddhists who emphasized the importance of *a direct intuitive insight as the transcendental truth,* beyond all intellectual conceptions. However, this insight can only come at times of mindfulness, when there is a connection with the true self. At the core of wabi-sabi is the importance of transcending learned ways of looking and thinking about things, even one's own existence. Specifically, according to the philosophy of wabi-sabi:

※ All things are impermanent,

※ All things are imperfect, and

※ All things are incomplete.

As an example, when we look at a tree, the lines in the bark, the tree's color, as well as the foliage, are all unique characteristics of that particular tree. Thus, each tree is uniquely beautiful. Similarly, the lines in a person's face are what lets us know how much they have laughed, thought deeply, experienced pain, or were kind to others. Wabi-sabi provides a philosophy that requires a mindful awareness and appreciation of our surroundings each moment.

Now let's get started. Allow yourself at least twenty minutes to take this type of walk. This is not a walk for physical exercise, and you can feel free to sit down at any time during this activity. The importance of this exercise is that you will have an opportunity to practice a walking meditation. Try taking such a walk at least once a week—perhaps for the rest of your life. As you go on this walk, engage in the following steps.

1. Begin by engaging in mindfulness breathing (see previous meditation tool).

2. As you breathe in, be aware that you are receiving life.

3. As you exhale, be aware that you are giving something back to the world.

4. Stay in the present.

5. Clear all thoughts of the past or future.

6. Stay in touch with your breathing.

7. As any thoughts come into your mind, simply observe them and let them pass.

8. Let any of these thoughts go and refocus on the present.

9. The purpose is to be present and aware of your breathing and walking.

10. Be aware of your feet as you walk, one foot in front of the other.

11. Walk gently on the earth. Be aware that with every step you are placing your footprint on the earth.

12. You can coordinate your breathing with your steps by taking an "in" breath every three or four steps, followed by an "out" breath every few steps. You may quietly whisper "in" and "out" to yourself as you go along your path.

13. Notice how your feet and legs are able to make each step with the needed amount of distance.

14. Be aware of all other sights, smells, and life in your surroundings—the car horns, the birds, the traffic noises, the leaves on a tree, the blades of grass, the concrete walkway, the park bench, or the mall parking lot.

15. Notice that everything you see is imperfect, impermanent, and incomplete. The tree's bark has cracks in it indicating its age or the conditions under which it grew. As you walk along the concrete path, you may notice that it is cracked, covered with leaves, debris, or animal droppings.

16. Be aware of people. Notice how imperfect, incomplete, or impermanent they are.

17. Visualize how you're connected to each person in some way or they to each other.

18. Be aware of the life and energy that's around you—the people, plants, and animals.

19. What is present in your surrounding that you cannot see? Perhaps a squirrel that is climbing on the other side of the tree, the pain experienced by the elderly gentleman who crosses the street with his cane, or the bulbs of spring flowers that are still under a frozen ground. Be aware that even though you may be aware of all that you observe, there are objects present that you cannot see with your eyes.

20. As you return from your walk, be aware of all those things that you may have missed on previous walks. Make a commitment to become more mindful as you go through your day in order that you may connect with your true essence and that of others in your future day-to-day travels.

The focus of this chapter on spiritual awareness thus far has been on the use of meditative activities, such as the mindfulness meditation tool and the wabi-sabi walk, to help calm and still your mind and to increase awareness of your basic spiritual essence. Now we'll move on to learning ways in which this awareness may help you in everyday life situations.

"LIFE" versus "Life"

Many terms have been used to represent this deep, basic, life force within each one of us. It has been referred to by many terms, including "soul," "spirit," "light," "universal energy," "eternal love," or the connection to God within each one of us. We find it helpful to use the word "LIFE" (using capital letters) to represent this basic spiritual essence, what we have been previously calling your "true essence."

This true essence, or LIFE, is what makes us all alive and connected to one another, not our daily circumstances, activities, or situations—what most people, in everyday language, refer to as "life." We believe that this is an important distinction to make as we go on our spiritual journey in the everyday world, as we need to attend to both our LIFE *and* our life.

At times, it may seem difficult to balance spiritual awareness and other spiritual goals with the day-to-day problems we face and the responsibilities we have to others. Indeed, we may view using our thought processes, which have often served to block us from our spiritual awareness, as useless in attaining our spiritual goals. Trying to solve problems, to establish goals for personal change, and to make plans for how to achieve these goals may at times seem inconsistent with a commitment to value the moment, accept our inner selves, and express gratitude for what is eternally present. However, ignoring problems or life situations that are causing you pain can be as detrimental to your spiritual journey as ignoring your inner essence. *There is nothing spiritually inconsistent with learning mindfulness while striving to improve your life situation.*

You will realize, as you increase your spiritual awareness, that life situations, activities, triumphs, and disappointments, are *not* your LIFE. As we noted earlier, your LIFE is that inner part of you, connected to the LIFE in every other living being, which is already perfect. Your life, on the other hand, has a constant supply of change, successes, failures, obstacles, losses, demands, and activities. What can deter you from your spiritual path is when you begin to mistake your life situation for your LIFE.

Becoming an Architect of Your Life Situations

To help better explain this difference, we would like to introduce a new metaphor, adapted from the words of a contemporary spiritual writer, Eckhart Tolle (1999). According to this metaphor, you picture your life as a large house. We suggest that you think of yourself as the architect of this house; that is, you designate where the house will be built, design what it will look like, and decide what building materials to use. You're largely responsible for how it will feel to be in the house, what aspects will be remembered, and what activities occur within the walls. In this way, the house will be unique among all other houses, just as your life is. However, the foundation of the house is that part that few may see but is critical to the house's overall stability.

In this metaphor, the actual house, the planning, building, and activities that occur within its walls represent your life. On the other hand, the foundation represents your LIFE. Spiritual awareness is crucial because to ignore it would be analogous to architects who ignore the foundation and expend all their energy on the above-ground structure and physical use of the house. No matter how attractive or large the house, if the foundation goes, so does the house.

As you become more aware or mindful of your present moments, you will notice that there are current life situations that require work or change. For example, with regard to your day-to-day activities, there may be skills that you want to improve, obstacles in your path, barriers to your personal goals, financial problems, lack of support, or even a direct assault from others. The next tool that we provide is designed to help you to begin to systematically approach these everyday problems so that you will eventually become more efficient and competent at solving them. This is important because as you become more competent at understanding and ultimately solving everyday problems, you allow more time for your continued spiritual growth. In other words, we believe that to reach your full potential, it's important to attend to both the house itself as well as the foundation.

Understanding Everyday Problems

The following are a series of steps to go through as a means of adopting a more "Zen-like" perspective regarding problems. In other words, because such problems are real and have direct effects on you, you need to attend to them. To help you cope more successfully with such problems, we will describe strategies that are based on the work of psychologists such as Tom D'Zurilla and ourselves (D'Zurilla and Nezu 1999; Nezu, Nezu, and Perri 1989). But don't forget the difference between LIFE and life.

Step 1: Stop and Be Aware

The first step to learning to better understand your everyday problems is to "Stop and be aware" of what is upsetting you. To carry out this step, visualize a stop sign or red traffic light when you first notice that you're experiencing distress, and repeat the following words to yourself: "I will stop and be aware of this life problem."

This step is important because creating the image of a red stop sign and giving yourself specific instructions can help stop you from complaining or feeling like a victim and impulsively reacting or trying to avoid the problem altogether. This step gives you the chance to figure out what your problem is *before* you act. We think of this as part of your "problem recognition radar." Learning to use this radar is important because it helps you to become more aware of the problems that you may want to work on and assists you in making decisions based upon a realistic view of the situation. After all, when our problem recognition is off, we all have a tendency to exaggerate or overestimate the problems we face.

You may find it useful to post this statement on the bathroom mirror or your refrigerator door to provide a constant reminder of the importance of learning to stop and be mindful of what is triggering your distress.

Consider the example of Mark, who was successfully completing his last semester in college. He looked forward to graduation and receiving his business degree. The time was coming soon when he would leave his close friendships at his fraternity house and return to his home in Chicago. He planned to stay with his parents until he found the advertising job he dreamed of.

As you place yourself in Mark's shoes and focus on the various thoughts and feelings that he might be experiencing, consider the range of possible reactions. If Mark was having difficulty recognizing problems, he might focus exclusively on the graduation parties, anticipate the great job he could possibly land in Chicago, daydream about the large salary he could earn, and anticipate being able to afford all of the things he wanted but couldn't get when he was a poor student. In essence, he might avoid thinking about all of the possible problems or obstacles that may occur and thus be unable to effectively handle them.

Some of these possible problems or obstacles might include hassles with regard to packing and moving all of his personal effects, having to say goodbye to his fraternity brothers, accepting greater responsibility regarding rent and home maintenance, possible conflicts that may arise when living with his parents again, having to make new social contacts, or the likely challenge of any job-hunting situation in the competitive advertising culture of Chicago. On the other hand, if Mark were hypersensitive to the existence of these problems and viewed them as overwhelming and insurmountable, focusing all attention on the likelihood of failure, he would also be faulty in his recognition and awareness. In this latter case, he might worry about never finding a job, anticipate his parents' disapproval of his failure, and become negatively preoccupied during the graduation activities, finding little pleasure in the successes and friendships he achieved at school.

In order for Mark to be more objective and accurate in his ability to recognize problems, it would be helpful if he used the strategies and tools from this chapter to increase his skills at both awareness of his LIFE and awareness of problems in life. The outcome of such efforts is that Mark will recognize first, through increased awareness of his LIFE, that none of the challenges he is facing will result in a basic change of his worth, value, or essence. However, Mark would also recognize that there are possible obstacles that may impede his plans for a successful life (for example, living in Chicago, being independent, and getting a job). These obstacles may trigger negative emotions, such as sadness (saying goodbye to friends and important sources of peer support), frustration (getting turned down for jobs), or anger (finding himself in a situation in which he is dependent upon his parents). When he can more accurately recognize and increase his awareness of these problems, he will be more able to move forward and engage in one of the following three options:

❧ To use his skills to change the nature of the situation or problem,

❧ To accept the problem and change the nature of any negative reactions to it, or

❧ To implement some combination of both.

Now bring your attention to your current everyday life. Make a list in your journal of all the potential areas you can think of in which you may experience life problems. Use the following headings to group problems together:

❧ Problems of health or well-being,

❧ Problems involving family,

❧ Problems involving work,

❧ Problems involving relationships with others,

❧ Problems involving leisure or quality time,

❧ Problems of a social nature, or

❧ Problems of a sexual nature.

Next, circle or underline areas that are *currently* a life problem for you. Afterward, circle or underline areas that are *potential* problems for you. We'll be using this information in the following steps.

Step 2: Remember that You Have Choices

Remind yourself that you have choices regarding what happens next in your life. Your choice will involve deciding to change the situation, accepting it, or discovering a way to combine these two choices.

Step 3: Define Your Problem

To help you to better define your problems, we ask you to respond to the following questions. Write the answers in your journal under the heading "What is the Problem?"

1. What makes this a problem for you?

2. What are the obstacles to overcome or the conflicts to resolve?

3. What are the things that need to change?

In answering these questions, be aware of your thoughts, feelings, and surroundings in order to try and get as much information about the problem as possible in order to better understand what is going on. In this situation, think of yourself as a police detective or scientist who is trying to get at the objective facts about the situation.

When you write down your answers, do so in clear language. For example, in describing a fearful situation, one person told us, "Riding in elevators is a nightmare. It's like I'm going to die. If the elevator doesn't kill me, the embarrassment will!" A more accurate and objective description, using clear language, would be, "My anxiety is at its most intense when I ride in an elevator. As soon as the doors open and I step inside, my heart beats faster, my skin gets clammy, I feel faint, and I have thoughts about dying. My thoughts are mostly focused on getting away." When we don't use clear and precise language, especially about problems, we can easily blow things out of proportion or have other people misunderstand what we're saying.

When you identify what makes the situation a problem for you, remember that the same life situation will present different levels of difficulty for different people. Even a minor hassle like getting to the airport can be very different for a student who is backpacking with little money as compared to a wealthy executive with a private chauffeur. Usually a problem occurs when a person is blocked in some way from getting what they want. This could be due to obstacles, conflicting goals, reduced resources, life situation changes, or actual losses.

Step 4: Set Realistic Goals

After identifying the problem, the next question to answer is what are your realistic goals for changing the situation? In other words, what do you want to see happen? What about the situation can change? What about you and your reaction to the situation can you change? In setting goals, remember to be realistic! Also, remember the choices you have for goals—to change the situation, your own negative reactions to it, or both.

Take out your journal and write down the answers to these questions. Remember to describe the facts in clear language. Writing in this way may very well allow you to think of possible ways to solve the problem.

Our clinical research over the past twenty-five years has indicated that most problematic life situations require changing *both* the nature of the situation that makes it problematic and our own reaction to the problem. There are many tools in this book that focus on changing or modifying our internal reactions to such problems, but changing the nature of the situation itself often means breaking it down into smaller parts. Bite-sized pieces help you set reachable goals and approach different parts of the problem one at a time.

Step 5: Practice Using this Tool

This tool can help you obtain a better understanding of your life's problems. In essence, it can help you become more aware of your life, identifying what changes are important to make. In other places throughout this book, we provide additional tools to help you change the nature of the situation so it's no longer a problem, change your negative emotional reactions to them, or both. For now, we wanted to help you to simply become more awake to such problematic life situations.

Increasing Joy

In this last section of this chapter, we offer a tool that can nurture both your life and your LIFE—increasing joy! As human beings, we are at our best when we experience joy. When we use the term "joy," we refer to a sense of delight, wanting to rejoice, and feeling gratitude for the moment. This type of experience is intensely personal, requires no justification, is unique to you, and may last only for a few moments. Joyful experiences are available to all of us, but we must be aware of them when they occur and practice cherishing their presence.

Even during difficult moments in our lives, instances of joy can occur. One example might be remembering the laughter and moments of fun you shared with a good friend who has just died. The loss of a friend is difficult, but the memory of laughter can create a moment of joy. While experiencing physical or emotional pain, you may find joy and gratitude in your connection to a helpful and supportive person. In that instant, you not only experience a shift in mood to the positive, but your body actually experiences biochemical changes that can be beneficial to your health. On the other hand, when we have only a few pleasant activities or lack joyful experiences, we feel depressed, burned out, bored, or sad. Our bodies experience fatigue. When we have these feelings, it's common to put off or even avoid doing things that bring us joy. This can increase feelings of sadness, contribute to the maintenance of depressive states, and disconnect us from LIFE.

One question that you may have is what comes first? Do we feel depressed and spiritually disconnected because we don't experience enough joy, or do we fail to seek out and create joyful experiences because we are depressed? The answer is that it seems to work in both ways. The less we do for ourselves, the more depressed we get, and the more depressed we get, the less we do. These negative feelings seriously impact our self-esteem because we view ourselves as undeserving of joy. Unfortunately, such lowered self-esteem and lack of pleasant or positive experiences can have very negative effects on our health. Studies show that our body systems, such as our immune and heart functioning, can be negatively affected by such feelings.

The good news is that there is a positive reversal to this downward spiral. There is a strong relationship between the number of positive or joyful experiences we create for ourselves and our mood. By increasing pleasant experiences, we feel better. This is important because, in addition to increasing our spiritual awareness, it gives us a useful means of controlling negative moods such as depression. This approach to treating depression was pioneered by psychologist Peter Lewinsohn and his colleagues (1978). The technique that they developed can help us to leave behind the self-defeating things that we have learned to say to ourselves and fosters our awareness of how best to increase our joyful experiences in our life situations (which can improve our LIFE!). Finally, we know that we are giving our bodies a gift that will increase the likelihood of positive effects on our physical health. By reducing depression, joyful experiences have been shown to have positive health benefits for our hearts and immune functioning, and can improve various stress-related medical conditions. According to the Bible, "The joyfulness of man prolongeth his days" (Psalms).

If you have been feeling sad, distressed, or burned out, it's likely that your rate of pleasant activities (big and small events that bring you a sense of joy) is low. You're not noticing pleasant experiences when they happen, not doing many of them, or not getting much pleasure from them when you do them. The purpose of this tool is to teach you:

❄ How to make a Joy Profile (list of the experiences and positive events that do bring you joy),

❄ How to become more aware of and notice positive, joyful experiences, and

❄ How to increase your Joy Profile (the frequency of pleasant activities and the extent to which you are enjoying them).

This is an effective tool for those who wish to feel happier, more satisfied, relaxed, interested, refreshed, and calm. Sometimes the effects of using this tool can be immediate. In addition, working with your Joy Profile can help you improve your awareness of who you are, what is truly important to you, and ultimately can have positive effects on your self-esteem. These effects often take a bit more time and should be combined with the other tools in the book to help achieve these more comprehensive goals.

Types of Activities

Although people differ regarding what experiences they find pleasant or joyful, there are a number of activities that psychologists, such as Lewinsohn have referred to as "mood-related activities" because they are strongly associated with how we feel. These activities are often divided into three categories: social activities, personal accomplishments, or "feel good" activities. They are described below.

Social Activities

These are activities through which people experience being enjoyed, respected, understood, valued, needed, supported, and loved by others. Some examples include being with someone who cares about how you feel, telling a joke, working on a project with a friend, caring for a child, and being asked your opinion.

Accomplishments

These are activities that give you a sense of achievement, satisfaction, individuality, success, or independence. Some examples include finishing a term paper, building a bookcase, writing a clever email, reading a book, or cooking a good meal.

"Feel Good" Activities

These are activities or experiences that "feel right" with regard to our inner spirit or our awareness of the joys in living. These include smelling baked bread, sweating during exercise, slipping into a hot tub, getting a backrub, watching a candle glow in a darkened room, or smelling the salty air at the seashore.

Creating Your Joy Profile

Plan on taking about thirty minutes to an hour to write down all the events, activities, experiences, and people in your life that you experience as pleasant or that typically bring you moments of joy. You should schedule an uninterrupted amount of time when you can concentrate on doing something important like this for yourself. At the end of this chapter, we provide sample lists of positive experiences that other people have identified. This may help you to create your own list, but remember to write down in your journal *only the things that truly apply to you.*

Step 1: Your List

Make a list in your journal of all the activities that you find pleasant. As a way of developing your own list, refer to the ones at the end of this chapter. These lists are a combination of ideas as described by psychologist Lewinsohn (for example, MacPhillamy and Lewinsohn 1982) and ones provided to us by many patients over the years who found them to be helpful. Look at each of the three lists. Write down in your journal those that appear right for you, even if you currently don't feel like doing any of them today. Think about additional ideas. Write down as many as you can think of. Make your list now.

Step 2: Your Experiences

Now go over the list and *underline* those positive activities that you actually did and experienced as joyful or pleasant. For example, suppose you wrote down "talk to my children" and actually had the opportunity to visit with your son or daughter or play with your grandchild last week. If you were able to enjoy this experience at the time, then underline it.

Step 3: Missed Opportunities

Now go back over the lists again and place an "X" next to the items that you actually experienced, but failed to be mindful of, take in fully, or enjoy. For example, maybe you took a nice, hot shower, an experience that you usually find pleasant, but were worried about something at work. Because you weren't able to stop and be mindful, you missed out on a pleasurable activity.

Step 4: Your Score

Add up the number of items that you wrote down. Now subtract the number of items that you underlined. This score is your Joy Profile. How many of the total number of the written items are you currently experiencing? If the number that you originally listed is close to or more than twice the number that you underlined, it's time to increase the joy in your life!

Also, look at the number of items marked "X." These are experiences that you're already experiencing but are missing out on because you are not mindful or attentive to them. It is time to discover the joys that are part of your life situation right now!

Making a Plan to Create More Joy

Step 1: Choose Some Pleasure

Following this plan may be one of the most important things you do for yourself. Look over the entire list one more time and think about the experiences that you could be having, but from which you are blocking yourself. Pick three items that you find pleasant and want to do more of—this may not be easy, because it may require some shifting of time and responsibilities. Write them down in your journal under the heading, "Make a Plan to Create More Joy."

Step 2: Commit to Awareness

In this step of the plan you will practice being more mindful of the beauty that you encounter in the present. Look at the items marked "X." Again, these are the activities that you actually experienced but failed to notice, take in, or enjoy. These are happening already, but unfortunately, you're not getting the full benefit of the joy they can give you. Therefore, write three items that you will make a commitment to notice and take in (things like your baby's smile, the friendly salesperson at the store, singing a song, lighting a candle at Shabbat, hugging your friend). Write them down in your journal.

Tracking Your Progress

Pick a time each week in which you will take a few moments to rate yourself on a scale of 1 to 10 ("1" being the worst and "10" being the best) regarding two questions:

❧ What is my overall level of spiritual awareness?

❧ What is my overall mood?

These ratings are not meant to be a rating of your awareness or emotions at any one specific time during the week. For example, in a given week, you may have cried because you missed a friend, experienced several new joyful experiences, become frustrated in traffic, or started to feel sick due to an impending cold. You may have been able to experience more joy in eating a good meal or helping a friend, but became preoccupied with angry or attacking thoughts during a disagreement with your spouse or partner. All of these events may involve different ratings. However, looking over the week *in general,* how would your rate your spiritual awareness and your mood? Monitor the direction and stability of your mood profile over several weeks. If you increase the quality of your mood, there's a good chance that the increase of your "joy quotient" is helping.

If your mood is *not* improving, continue to add three more activities each week to your list—and do them! Also look at the activities that you marked with an "X" and take the time to enjoy them more. Plan to allow a few extra moments to notice how pleasant the experience is—focus your attention and mindfulness on this joyful experience.

It's important to remember that no matter how disconnected, depressed, or hopeless you feel, there are always some activities and thoughts that are pleasant, even for a fleeting moment. If you find yourself saying that you're too busy, too burned out, or undeserving to take the time to construct your joy profile, then this tool is *precisely* what you need to help you to begin to transform yourself. Remember, don't just look for joy, *create it!* In addition, as the Roman orator Seneca said centuries ago, "Learn to feel joy!"

Summary

In this chapter we've introduced tools to help make your first steps on this journey a little easier and provided a means by which to map out your unique journey to awakening your self-esteem. Our goal was to help you foster your own spiritual self-awareness in order to be "awake" during your journey. As part of enhancing your spiritual awareness, you can use the several tools you learned to foster your ability to "stay in the moment" in order to be in better touch with your true essence and desired spiritual goals. As you proceed on your journey, remember the distinction between LIFE and life, and that it's important to attend to both areas, just as you would make sure that both your house and its foundation are taken care of. Also take the opportunity to increase your joy, as happiness helps both.

Having your travel itinerary and your "light" (that is, your enhanced spiritual awareness), you are now ready to start off on the journey towards awakening self-esteem. The tools that you've already learned (for example, visualization, mindfulness meditation, creating joy) *can be used on any leg of your travels,* not just to get started. But please be sure that you practice the tools in these first two chapters, as they will greatly affect the overall quality of your journey. Your journey may take a long time. There is a part of you that already knows that it is a lifelong process, although you can reach your spiritual goals by reading the remainder of the book within weeks or months. But once you reach your final destination, you will probably realize that, just like many journeys you've taken before, you will want to go back.

So, have a great trip. Take out your travel itinerary and go to those destinations that are important to you. Some may lead to the very next chapter, while others may mean stopping at one of the further chapters in order to enhance, for example, their ability to be forgiving or patient. Still others may go straight to chapter 9, the final chapter. But that's up to you. Take your journey, be educated and enlightened, and enjoy.

Table 2. List of Positive Experiences

Social Activities

Being with friends	Being with people with similar interests
Being helped with something	Having an honest conversation
Discussing something interesting	Going to a party
Meeting someone new	Going to a church, temple, shrine, or mosque
Going to a music concert, ballet, or theater	Going to a convention
Going to a sports event	Playing with children
Going to a race (horse, car, or boat)	Going to a fair, carnival, or zoo
Going walking, hiking, camping	Talking about philosophy, morals, or religion
Playing cards or board games	Dating
Being at a wedding, bar mitzvah, baptism, graduation, or birthday party	Having a cup of coffee, cup of tea, cocktail, glass of wine or beer with someone
Playing tennis, golf, or other sport	Having lunch with someone that you like

Visiting someone shut in
(hospital, rehab, prison)

Planning or organizing an
event

Talking on the telephone

Going to the movies

Giving gifts

Getting letters or cards

Going to an outdoor event

Buying something for your
family

Talking to your children or
grandchildren

Being told that you are
needed

Giving a party

Visiting friends

Having sexual relations

Talking about hobbies or
interests

Watching attractive men or
women

Smiling at people

Expressing your love to
someone

Expressing your appreciation
to someone

Going to an auction or sale

Hearing a good sermon or
speech

Being complimented

Seeing good things happen to
your family or friends

Having a friend come to visit

Going to a reunion

Kissing or hugging

Going to school or class

Introducing people to each
other

Sending letters or cards or
notes

Helping someone

Loaning something

Being at a family get-together

Coaching someone

Being invited out

Having someone agree with
you

Finding out about someone's
joy or sorrow

Giving a massage or back rub

Being counseled

Talking to people at work

Doing things with children

Doing volunteer work

Seeing old friends

Accomplishments

Making a contribution to a charity organization

Playing a sport

Doing artwork

Redecorating your room or home

Driving skillfully

Boating

Working on your computer

Completing a difficult task

Writing a story, poem, novel, or play

Exploring unknown places

Speaking a foreign language

Cooking

Solving a personal problem

Playing pool, billiards, or bowling

Having an original idea

Learning a new skill

Taking photographs

Reading a map

Making a major purchase

Hearing a joke

Eating a good meal

Writing a letter, paper, or essay

Fishing

Doing heavy outdoor work

Completing a crossword puzzle

Running, jogging, or walking

Having a debate

Being prepared for a test or job

Planning a trip or vacation

Hiking or climbing

Going to a lecture

Singing

Restoring antiques

Tinkering with cars or other machines

Solving a problem or puzzle

Writing a note to someone

Working at your job

Playing a musical instrument

Skiing

Making food or crafts to give away

Weighing yourself

Gardening or landscaping

Competing at sports

Giving a speech or lecture

Washing clothes

Getting a promotion at work

Winning a bet

Hunting

Horseback riding

Doing a project in your own way

Reading a paper

Swimming

Playing catch

Making people laugh

Doing needlework

Building a fire

Using your strength

Waterskiing, surfing, or scuba diving

Receiving money

Winning a competition

Starting a new project

Teaching someone

Preparing special food

Hanging laundry outside to dry

Defending or protecting someone

Making my Joy Profile

"Feel Good" Activities

Being in the country

Buying or picking flowers for yourself

Watching the ocean

Being at the beach

Reading stories, novels, poems, or plays

Thinking about something good in the future

Giving your opinion or advice

Shaving

Taking a long car trip

Riding in an airplane

Holding a baby

Being in a sporty car

Taking a nap

Combing or brushing your hair

Watching someone you love

Being in a city

Putting on make-up

Wearing new clothes

Getting dressed up

Buying something for yourself

Giving something away

Reading spiritual or religious writings

Watching TV

Laughing

Hugging

Taking a shower or bath

Being with an animal or pet

Prayer or meditation

Lighting or watching candles

Crying

Wearing casual clothes

Driving fast

Singing to yourself

Looking at the stars or moon

Watching an animal

Dancing

Sitting in the sun	Riding a motorcycle
Sitting and being mindful	Gambling
Listening to nature sounds	Listening to the radio or records
Getting a massage	Getting ice cream
Thinking about people you like	Noticing that you smell good
Having daydreams	Kicking leaves
Making popcorn	Being alone
Feeling the presence of spiritual forces	Renting a video
Washing your hair	Going to a restaurant
Getting up early	Getting up late
Reminiscing	Writing in a diary
Practicing yoga	Sleeping soundly
Going to a hair salon	Reading magazines
Going to a library or bookstore	Sitting in a café
Bird watching	Beach combing
Eating snacks	Going to a health club or spa
Going to a museum	Working on your Joy Profile

PART II

Journey Destinations: Spiritual Goals

CHAPTER 3

Enhancing Relationships

Like the body that is made up of different limbs and organs,
all mortal creatures exist depending upon one another.

—Hindu Proverb

The Spiritual Goal of Enhancing Relationships

Enhancing relationships and opening our hearts in connection with others is a common spiritual goal. Despite superficial differences in appearance, age, race, gender, or skill levels, people are equal in their basic worth as human beings. Despite this diversity, one way in which we are very similar involves our mutual desire for affiliation and connection with each other. In the same way that enhancing our spiritual awareness helps to connect us with true essence, focusing our awareness about our relationships can facilitate our connection to others. This human connection inspires people toward compassion and is a prime example of a core tenet of Zen Buddhism known as *sunyata*, which suggests that everything, including people, are interconnected.

> The source of all misery in the world lies
> in thinking of oneself; the source of all
> happiness lies in thinking of others.
>
> —Shantideva

Connection: One Path to Self-Esteem

As the Dalai Lama has observed, when we are focused on this human connection and learn to nurture the relationships in our lives, we experience an increase in our sense of worth and dignity. After all, what can be more worthwhile than the opportunity to make a meaningful contribution to someone else's life? This is how the spiritual goal of enhancing our relationships can lead to awakening self-esteem. When we focus on our relationship with others, we're less concerned about our own self-worth. As we think about how we can be helpful to someone else, such as a child, spouse, life partner, or friend, our vital essence becomes enhanced. Connectedness helps not only our spiritual advancement and self-esteem, but it enhances our happiness as well.

People who experience low self-esteem often report feelings of dissatisfaction or discontent with personal relationships. This is not surprising, in that many scientific studies have documented the significant role that socially supportive experiences play in lessening our distress in difficult life situations, including times of illness, loss, and anxiety. The presence of another person who believes in our worth, validates our emotions, and listens to our concerns is a precious gift. The tools in this chapter are geared to help you to give and receive such gifts in order to enhance your relationships.

Common Obstacles to Connection

It's often difficult for people to connect with others, especially during times of stress, when most of us focus instead on preserving our self-esteem or comparing ourselves with others. Envy, jealously, anger, anxiety, and hopelessness are the by-products of our fears about our own worth and value, and such emotions can be very destructive to our relationships. When we have doubts about our own worth, we often withdraw from the very people we usually enjoy spending time with. When we do this, we miss out on the benefits of social support. We can get so busy thinking about how we look, what we do, how much we earn, how smart we are, how many books we have written, how attractive or funny we are, or how strong we are that we ignore or block out the connection to those close to us.

Has this ever happened to you? Have you ever had people near to your heart tell you that your feelings of fear, jealousy, anger, withdrawal, or sadness are interfering with their relationship with you? Perhaps you've said these words to someone else who you believe is behaving destructively. When a person exerts so much mental focus on themselves, they tend to remain hyper-vigilant and selective to any information that may signal a threat of their struggle for acceptance or worthiness. In other words, we are so busy trying to protect our self-esteem that we ignore or even hurt the people who are trying to connect with us.

In this chapter, you will be introduced to tools that can help you to think more accurately, experience the emotions of others through empathy and compassion, and get the support you need. Such skills can provide you with much greater opportunities and likelihood of connecting with others. We will start with a tool that helps you to recognize and change negative thinking habits that often get in the way of true connection.

Negative Thinking Habits

Negative thinking habits are patterns of destructive thoughts that lead to unpleasant and strong emotional reactions. It's important to understand the less than helpful ways you've learned to think and then to "unlearn" these thinking patterns, as they block you from connecting with other people. Continuous negative thinking can drive people away from you or can prevent you from working on developing a positive connection with another person.

The Big 3

The particularly destructive thought habits that, as psychologists, we refer to as "The Big 3" are fearful thoughts, hostile thoughts, and depressive thoughts. These thoughts are so destructive to your psychological, emotional, and physical health that they have been associated, either individually or in combination, to all variants of psychological illness and behavioral disorders, as well as aggression, assault, murder, suicide, heart disease, disorders of immune functioning, pain syndromes, substance abuse, and power struggles between couples, families, communities, and countries. This list sounds like a plague of biblical proportions! By now, you probably have an idea how important we think it is to work on changing these habits because they will interfere with your spiritual goal of connecting with others and negatively affect your sense of well-being.

Thinking habits can trigger distressful and unpleasant emotions because the way in which people perceive and interpret various events in their life situations determines to a large degree their consequent emotional and physical reactions. If you interpret a situation as negative (for example, seeing it as fearful, hostile, sad, or hopeless), then your resulting emotional reaction is also likely to be negative. Conversely, if your interpretation is more positive and realistic, then the emotional reaction is more likely to be positive and realistic. All negative thinking habits distort the truth and lack accuracy (see also the tool in chapter 9 called "Separating Facts from Assumptions"). Let's examine the specific characteristics and consequences of the Big 3 negative thinking habits.

Fearful Thinking

When people are caught in a fearful thinking habit, they become prisoners to all that they fear. They block their awareness of their own spirit and LIFE. Because they are engaged in fearful thinking, much of their energy is focused on avoiding the unpleasant aspects of anxiety. To use a sports analogy, it's as if they came onto the playing field with strategies focused on *avoiding loss* rather than on trying to win. Any sports fan will know that to increase your chances of winning, a player must hit a ball, run a distance, make a catch, or outrun a tackle. The main point is that the player must be willing to get a few bumps and bruises, navigate obstacles, and come up against blocks along the way. In order to win, you must play to win, rather than play to avoid losing. Fearful thinking results in a type of self-imprisonment where you are stuck in a cycle of avoidance. Your thoughts encourage you to live like a child hiding from a bully—you can hide for a time, but you will never be able to stand out in the open. Of course in the case of fearful thinking, you are your own worst bully.

Many patients have asked us why they have learned to think this way. The immediate answer that comes to mind is "you learned to." But, that's not as simple as it sounds. Learning is a very complicated process. First, you may have a predisposition or tendency to have stronger or quicker internal reactions than others. In other words, the unpleasantness or discomfort you feel when afraid may engender more physical reactivity than what someone else experiences. Another reason may be that your parents, caregivers, siblings, peers, or other influential people in your life have communicated, either intentionally or not, that certain types of emotional or physical distress are *intolerable* or represents something *terrible*. In such a case, you've learned that the experience of fear itself is something to be avoided. Finally, our brains appear to be hard-wired to have us learn to be afraid, as avoidance of true life-threatening events is very adaptive. As human beings, we have a very well-tuned brain network to help us avoid true danger. The problem is that, through many different types of conditioning or learning, we come to respond to many different situations, thoughts, and experiences as dangerous. For example, the dangers of failure, humiliation, embarrassment, or even negative feelings are circumstances that we learn to avoid. It doesn't matter whether or not anyone intentionally taught you to think fearfully, but due to the circumstances of your development, you learned how.

Identifying Fearful Thoughts

In order to change your fearful thoughts, you will have to be able to use your awareness skills to catch yourself stating fear-based statements silently to yourself. Another way to state this is for you to "be mindful" of your fearful thoughts. Common fear-based thoughts contain an anticipation of harm. Examples include when you hear yourself making internal statements that you may fail at something important or that other people may get angry with you. Thoughts like these indicate that your mind would prefer you to avoid a situation you can't control. If you follow through with avoidance, you'll escape from possible negative results—but you'll also miss out on many positive experiences.

Another common fearful thought involves assuming what others think (or "mind-reading") when you have no proof. Examples of these fearful thoughts include "He thinks I'm stupid," "They're probably laughing at me," "I'm boring to her," or "He doesn't care about me." Have you ever experienced thoughts like these? In such cases, your mind may be trying to exert a false sense of control over the situation. In other words, if you can be sure about the other person's negative reaction, you won't have to cope with an unknown. Your mind has already reasoned that if you expect love and approval from others, but are disappointed, that would be devastating. Following this logic, it's better to just accept the worst now.

Hostile and Cynical Thoughts

It may sound like a paradox, because most of us don't think of hostile people as scared or frightened, but hostile thoughts are actually quite similar to fearful thoughts. The hostile or overbearing person who intimidates others has learned to intentionally "stack the deck" in their favor so the other guy will always get the criticism, disapproval, or abuse—another way to avoid any unpleasant experiences of failure, imperfection, or lack of control. The difference with hostile thoughts versus fearful thoughts is the content. Specifically, the content of hostile thoughts is other people, where people are blamed for disappointments and viewed as foolish. When you engage in hostile thinking, your mind tells you that others don't respect you and don't give you the proper credit you're due. In short, they don't recognize how "great" you are. You have learned that by seeing others as stupid or faulty, you don't have to look at any faults or problems of your own. To focus on yourself is seen as too threatening and likely to engender very unpleasant emotions. You've learned that it's better to engage in hostile thinking, keep such emotions away, and perceive yourself as in control. The problem is that these thinking errors can harm your relationships and your emotional and physical well-being.

Although individuals who have hostile thinking habits are less likely to see a therapist and seek help in changing, many do, either because their partner or family has asked them to, or they have experienced a legal, financial, medical, or personal setback due to their hostile thinking or angry behavior. Because of the association between hostile thinking and specific medical conditions such as hypertension and cardiac arrhythmia, many people are referred for help in changing their hostile thinking by their physicians. Perhaps one of these situations applies to you. In any event, you may be asking yourself how people with problems of hostility learn to have these thinking habits.

If you have a tendency toward hostile thoughts, perhaps you were rewarded for being strong, independent, or tough, and thinking of yourself in that way helped you avoid unpleasant feelings or insecurities. Perhaps you were punished harshly for minor faults or mistakes and learned to tell yourself that such characteristics should be punished in others. Perhaps you were spoiled by your parents and they could not bear to see you upset. As such, you had to always find a reason why you should not or could not accept responsibility for the periodic problems and distress that are experienced by all human beings. As you can see, there might be several ways that people learn to think in a hostile manner.

Identifying Hostile Thoughts

Hostile thoughts are pretty easy to identify if you're attentive and want to learn how to catch yourself. They often take the form of name-calling of others in your head, for example, "That idiot," "You moron," or "What a witch." Your mind is making sure that all blame for any experienced distress goes squarely on the shoulders of the other person. In this way you don't have to deal with feeling bad, recognizing your faults, or changing anything you do.

Another common hostile thought process is identified by your interpretation of any disappointment as directed personally toward you. For example, if someone's actions disappoint you, you assume that their behavior is the result of a direct attempt to hurt or insult you. This thinking habit, referred to "personalization," is described in detail in the chapter on forgiveness (chapter 6) later in the book, as so many people who experience difficulty with forgiveness also have hostile thinking habits. If you have particular difficulties or trouble forgiving others, you may wish to go to chapter 6 after completing this chapter in order to learn more about personalization and other techniques to help you with forgiveness.

Your mind has learned that hostile thoughts can keep away any responsibility for personal failures, problems, or imperfections of behavior that you have. As in the case with fearful thoughts, the desire to have such complete control over imperfections in your life is impossible, and the need to desperately protect your value and human worth from any faults is unnecessary. Remember that in a spiritual sense, your LIFE or vital essence, is *already* perfect. Your human attributes and life situations may have many weaknesses and imperfections, but, spiritually speaking, you're just fine.

Depressive Thinking

When you're absorbed in depressive thinking, your mind is telling you that you are defective, inferior, or that you have no value. You tend not to engage in as many fearful or hostile mind habits with yourself because you're convinced that the reason things are unlikely to work out or result in your feeling happy is because of you! You don't believe that you can control the outcome by blaming someone else or avoiding the situation, as you're sure that nothing much will turn out well, that you are likely to fail, that all your vulnerabilities will be revealed, and that you're unlikely to experience any pleasure or enjoyment in your life. Whereas fearful and hostile thinking block out the spiritual awareness of your LIFE, depression tries to extinguish it with hopelessness. When people are chronically and severely hopeless, they may occasionally succeed at extinguishing their LIFE through acts of self-destruction or suicide. Many spiritual philosophies would argue that while it is possible to end your life, it is impossible to extinguish your LIFE.

Identifying Depressive Thought

Depressive thoughts can be identified by their exaggerated, overmagnified, and overgeneralized nature. On such occasions, your mind is finding a small and isolated grain of negative truth but making it huge. For example, problematic life situations such as getting reprimanded at work, receiving a failing grade on a test, experiencing a disagreement with a family member, gaining weight, or receiving criticism, are viewed by the depressive mind as catastrophic, terrible, devastating, enduring, and all-encompassing phenomena. These are the easiest depressive distortions to recognize; for example, "I was devastated by receiving that rejection letter." The more subtle and difficult depressive thinking patterns occur when our life is such that many other people may share or reinforce the exaggerated or distorted thoughts. One example involves times when you're confronted with trauma or illness. When working with breast-cancer survivors, we have heard common reactions that included thoughts such as, "A mastectomy? No one will ever find me attractive sexually." Another example of depressive thinking is experienced by men who have been laid off from their jobs, statement like, "I've lost job. I'm no longer a man. I can't take care of my family."

In situations like these, the recognition of depressive thinking is clearly more difficult because people are facing truly frightening and challenging life situations. However, the depressive thinking in both of these examples is inaccurate and likely to work against the person's efforts to manage their difficult life circumstances. In the first case, a woman facing cancer treatment, surgery, and all the post-surgical decisions will be experiencing real fear, pain, confusion, and uncertainty. Her relationships may change. Her lifestyle will be greatly impacted. But look carefully at the thought we described. Notice that she is making specific assumptions that are enduring, generalized, and hopeless. A more accurate thought may be, "A mastectomy? I am about to experience a very difficult and challenging time in my life with many problems in front of me." With the second statement, a similar change to more accurate thinking can also be applied. In this situation, the thinker is making statements equating his own challenging life situation with his very value as a human being and a man. How can this thinking serve any purpose but to choke any desires he may have to seek help and support? If he begins to believe he has lost his value as a man, how can he ask for help and support from his wife and friends? We could predict that he would view himself as unworthy of their love and support, and a downward spiral would ensue. A more accurate thought would be, "I want to be able to provide for my family. I am feeling frustrated, disappointed, and guilty. This makes it even more difficult for me to work on a plan to get through this."

Learning to Confront Your Negative Thinking

Unless you confront your negative thinking, you are likely to become hopeless as you react to the presence of such thoughts as evidence of how your life will not improve. Although negative thinking is unpleasant, it is not hopeless. Through techniques of cognitive therapy pioneered by psychiatrist Aaron T. Beck, many people have successfully learned to change their negative thoughts. This approach basically suggests that how we feel is often determined by what we think (Beck 1993). We will provide some insights from this type of therapy approach to help you better understand and change your own negative thinking.

Remember the last time that you were embarrassed, sad, fearful, or angry? You remained the same person—had the same LIFE—even though your mind was preoccupied with fearful, hostile, or depressive thoughts. The good news is that you can change these thoughts while maintaining the "real" you. It is important to remember that your mind has learned these negative thinking patterns. As we have stated previously, negative thinking habits can often contribute to anxiety, anger, and depression. Learning to change your negative thinking can have a significant impact on many areas of your life situation—your mood, your relationships, and the things you do for yourself and others. These things, in turn, allow you to fully experience your LIFE.

As an example of how different thoughts can lead to different emotions, consider the "ABC" way of understanding how thoughts affect emotions. Imagine for a moment that you are getting home late from work and waiting at the checkout line at the supermarket. Now picture the following event (we will label this event "A"). Someone behind you bumps into your legs with their cart, almost causing you to fall. What thoughts may come into your mind (we will label such thoughts, "B")? Now imagine the different emotional reactions (we will label these emotions "C") that might occur as a result of the various types of thoughts, "B." As contained in the list below, notice how your interpretation of the same event might create very different emotional reactions. In other words, what "B" (or a thought) is, even if "A" (or the event) is the same, determines the resulting "C" (or consequent emotional reaction), rather than the actual nature of the event ("A") itself. If A = You are bumped from behind, note the varying emotional consequences resulting from the differing types of thoughts:

If B = "Hey! That hurt! He did that on purpose!"
  then C = Anger

If B = "Nobody cares about me,"
  then C = Sadness

If B = "This guy will be rude and hassle me,"
  then C = Fear

If B = "Hey, it's my friend Joe playing around!"
  then C = Amusement

If B = "Maybe it's that blind man I noticed coming down the aisle—hope he's all right,"
  then C = Concern.

Using the following tool, developed by cognitive therapists Dennis Greenberger and Christine Padesky (1995), you can learn how to make more accurate interpretations in order to help change your automatic negative thoughts. This tool works like putting on a pair of glasses to help you see things more clearly. Remember that cognitive therapy techniques have been repeatedly shown to improve both mood and behavior (Beck 1993).

Right now, take out your journal, and think about the last time that you were upset. Write down three of your most troublesome thoughts. Confronting your troubling thoughts may be uncomfortable, but try staying with the exercise and write them down. Allow yourself to say them silently in your head and just observe them, notice them, much in the way you became aware of your thoughts when you practiced the mindfulness breathing mediation in chapter 2. These are thoughts that your mind has learned to say. Any of them may meet the definition of fearful, depressive, or hostile thoughts. In a few moments, you will be able to return to them and determine how accurate they really are. For now, we'd like you to make a commitment to try and change these thinking habits.

All three of the negative thinking habits that we discussed are based upon self-talk (or what our minds have learned to say). Negative self-talk is usually automatic and, similar to assumptions, isn't based on facts. At best, it's based on a distortion of a few selected facts. Many times these distortions are made so we can tell ourselves that we have some control over a threatening or challenging situation. For example, if a person discovers a partner's unfaithfulness and makes a general conclusion such as "all men are untrustworthy" or "I will never be happy," their minds are hard at work determining a "rule" to live by so they won't have face the same threat in the future. The problem is that these are the types of distortions that lead to huge thinking errors.

When a perspective is distorted and narrow, it becomes very difficult to see the whole picture and understand both negative *and* positive aspects of a situation accurately. Such thinking is certainly not unique. Remember that many people engage in negative thinking. The important point here is to commit yourself to unlearning negative thought patterns and start thinking in a more objective and accurate way. It's important to change these patterns because such thoughts lead to negative emotional reactions and can inhibit your ability to connect with other people. You already experience your share of emotional pain when your thinking is accurate and you experience stressful life situations. Why create additional distress based upon distorted thoughts?

In order to successfully change your negative thinking patterns, you need to first be able to monitor your negative thoughts. In other words, you need to have a way of understanding what is going on with your own thinking. Here is where the Thought Record can be useful.

Using Your Thought Record

A *Thought Record* is basically a piece of paper divided into three sections. You can use your journal to create yours. In each section, there is specific information to write down.

1. First, what is the situation or event that happened just before you felt badly?

2. Next, write down what feelings you experienced and how bad those feelings were on a scale of 0 to 10 (where 0 = not bad at all and 10 = very bad).

3. In the last section, list your automatic thoughts. This takes some practice and it will be helpful to use the questions we have listed later in the chapter to tap into these thoughts. After writing these thoughts down, you will notice that some are connected to very strong feelings—cognitive therapists refer to these as "hot" thoughts. Circle any "hot" thoughts that you have listed.

Here is an example of a Thought Record filled out by a patient.

> ## Joe's Thought Record
>
> 1. **Situation:** *Getting ready for a family party and thinking about seeing my older brother, Sam.*
>
> 2. **Mood:** *Angry = 9; Sad = 7*
>
> 3. **Thoughts:** *Memories of my father talking about how smart my brother is* (hot thought); I'm the family loser, everybody likes my brother Sam; An old image of my father looking at me with disappointment; I don't want to go to this stupid picnic with my messed-up family.*

As you can see, Joe is feeling very poorly. However, he now has a better understanding of why family parties are difficult for him and why he has difficulty connecting with others. Notice how the mood and thoughts section separate out the thoughts and feelings that he is experiencing from the section describing the situation. After you have learned how to keep a Thought Record, you will be ready to use the tool to change your negative thoughts. You will get the best results if you use the following strategy to practice changing your negative thinking at least once daily. Remember that you are using a very powerful tool and it's worth the practice!

Changing Your Negative Thinking Patterns

Changing negative thinking habits involves much more than just thinking positively. It means practicing looking at a situation more accurately from new and different perspectives. By looking at a situation from many different perspectives (this includes positive, negative, and neutral sides), you will develop more accurate conclusions and ideas about the situation. You can use the Thought Record to guide you in changing your thinking habits. By expanding your form to include four more sections, it now becomes a Changing-Your-Thoughts Record, based on the work of Greenberger and Padesky (1995), and should include the following seven sections:

1. Situation

2. Mood

3. Hot Thoughts

4. Evidence in Support of Thoughts

5. Evidence Not in Support of Thoughts

6. Balanced Thoughts

7. Final Mood Rating (after completion of thought record)

Develop a form with the seven sections in your journal and follow the steps below to change negative thinking.

« *Step 1.* Create a Changing-Your-Thoughts Record form. Use this form at least once a day when you experience any negative emotions. Such feelings of distress may be mild (for example, you find yourself mildly irritated in traffic) or very intense (for example, you find yourself depressed following the breakup of a relationship).

« *Step 2.* Notice that this form starts with the same three sections that you used in the basic Thought Record. However, there are now four additional sections on the Changing-Your-Thoughts Record, two of which provides you with space to write down evidence both for *and* against the hot thoughts.

« *Step 3.* After writing down the situation, moods, mood rating, and automatic thoughts (don't forget to circle your hot thoughts), write down any factual evidence that you think can support the first hot thought that is circled. In actuality, you will find that getting evidence to support your hot thoughts isn't that easy. That's because many negative thoughts are based upon assumptions, not facts, and at times can be irrational or illogical.

« *Step 4.* Next, write down the evidence that you can find that goes against your hot thoughts. Finding evidence that does not support your hot thoughts requires your willingness to see another side. Ask family and friends for help—they can often provide such evidence because they are seeing a different side of the situation.

In addition, here are some questions that you can ask yourself as a way to help you find evidence against these hot thoughts:

Hot-Thought Questions

❈ Are there any experiences that I can identify to show that this thought is not completely true all the time?

❈ If my best friend had this very same thought, what would I tell them?

❈ What would my best friend or someone who loves me unconditionally say to me to help me understand that this thought is not 100 percent true?

❈ What would _____ (God, Jesus, Mohammed, Buddha, or someone currently living whom you respect for their wisdom and insight) say to me to help me recognize that this self-statement is not 100 percent true?

❈ Do I ever think differently about this situation when I am not feeling this way (many women, for example, describe heightened emotional sensitivity dependent upon their menstrual cycle)?

❈ Five years from now, if I look back on this situation, will I look at it differently?

❈ Are there strengths or positives in me in this situation that I am ignoring?

❈ Am I jumping to any conclusions that are not completely backed up by the facts of this situation?

❈ Am I blaming myself for something that is in the past?

❈ Am I blaming myself for something over which I have little or no control?

You will notice that the questions we provided are not designed to give you false positive statements to argue with your hot thoughts, but to help you think more *accurately*.

❈ *Step 5.* Now try to come up with more balanced thoughts about this situation—ones that are neither very negative or strongly arguing against the negative thoughts, but describing facts about the situation that you might not have written down before. Often more balanced thoughts arise when trying to find evidence against your negative thoughts.

❈ *Step 6.* Repeat these balanced thoughts to yourself. They are more accurate descriptions of the situation.

❰❰ *Step 7.* Stop to notice how you're feeling. Once again, rate your negative feelings after using the Changing-Your-Thoughts Record.

Let's get back to Joe. Here is an example of how his Changing-Your-Thoughts Record looks after he filled in all the remaining sections.

Joe's Changing-Thoughts Record

1. **Situation:** *Getting ready for a family party and thinking about seeing my older brother, Sam.*

2. **Mood:** *Angry = 9; Sad = 6*

3. **Hot Thoughts:** *"I'm a loser. Everybody likes Sam more than me."*

4. **Evidence in Support of Thoughts:** *I have not been as successful in a professional career or making money as my brother. I'm divorced, and I made many mistakes in my first marriage.*

5. **Evidence Not in Support of Thoughts:** *I have a good job. I have a good relationship with my son. I learned from the mistakes I made in my first marriage. I'm a talented guitarist. My brother has told me that he enjoys doing things with me. My parents never valued my music ability—they focused more on how much money someone makes as a measure of success. My parents' opinions are not necessarily true, nor are the opinions of everyone else.*

6. **Balanced Thoughts:** *We each have our strengths. My brother seems to enjoy my company! One goal for me is to stop attacking my brother for my parents' opinions.*

7. **New Mood Rating:** *Angry = 2; Sad = 3*

Let's now look at the mood ratings at the end of the Changing-Your-Thoughts Record exercise. Notice that Joe still has some negative feelings. These are reflected by the fact that his parents probably contributed to his negative views of himself when they did not value his talents. However, his mood is much improved, and he may actually develop positive social experiences with his brother that eventually serve more as a support than a threat. Here, Joe has learned that his negative thinking previously prevented him from having a close relationship with his brother. By reducing such thinking, he was able to focus more on fostering such a relationship.

Changing Your Negative Thoughts

When we first introduced this tool, we asked that you write down three of your most troubling thoughts. Write them down once again in your journal. Now see if you can recognize if any or all of these are fearful, angry, or depressive thoughts. Consider one that you have recently experienced. Create a Thought Record about that life situation, remembering to rate your mood as best as you can recall during the moment when you last experienced this thought in a real-life situation. Now create a Changing-Your-Thoughts Record concerning this thought, remembering to use the list of questions provided as a way of gaining accurate information that do *not* support the thought. Become aware of your feelings after repeating the balanced thoughts to yourself and rate your mood.

How To Track Your Progress

By continuing to use a Changing-Your-Thoughts Record, you can keep track of your progress by monitoring and noting your mood ratings using the scale from 1 to 10. If you experience any progress, don't forget to congratulate yourself! If you note a lack of positive change, you may be experiencing your current feelings as overwhelming. If so, try using this tool in combination with other tools in this book, such as those focused on calming your feelings, in order to help you think more clearly. Don't forget to reward yourself for trying, and remember that some improvement may result immediately, but big improvement comes with repeated use!

Thou shalt love thy neighbor as thyself.

—The Bible (Leviticus)

Developing Empathy and Compassion Skills

Empathy is one of the most important skills in helping you increase the quality of your relationships. When you experience empathy for another person, you experience what they are feeling. This is somewhat different than sympathy, in which you are able to *understand* what someone else is going through or can express your own feelings for another. Empathic understanding involves, in a sense, being able to see the world through someone else's eyes. Think of the last time you were moved by a powerful emotion while watching a movie. Were you simply reacting to a consideration of what the movie's character was going through, or could you find yourself catching glimpses of the world through their eyes? That moment, in which you experienced the character's feelings and experienced actual physical reactions as if you were going through the event yourself, was empathy. You may have experienced feelings of sadness or pain, or feelings of surprise, delight, or relief.

The reason why you were able to experience or share such feelings along with the character on the screen involves something about the scene that triggered your own feelings. At some point in time, you had experienced something similar. Even though the specific situation may be different, the *feeling* was similar.

When you're able to see the world through another's eyes and experience what they feel, you are often compelled to do what you can to relieve their suffering. This tendency to personally respond to reduce suffering in others takes empathy one step further and defines compassion. We think of empathy as an experience and compassion as an urge to act on your empathy.

When you are working hard to understand the experience of others, your attention is shifted away from your own insecurities or fears and you are directing your energy to emotionally care for someone else. When you accept compassionate actions as part of your purpose, you increase your self-esteem. Each act of compassion gives you evidence of your value as a human being.

The tools that follow are designed to help you to improve your own empathic ability. Anytime that you can search your own history for feelings that are similar to those of people around you, you will be sharpening your own "emotional radar" and increasing your ability to connect with others.

Empathy Skills Training: Your Library of Feelings

Search your own life history as if it were a reference library of emotions. Go through the following list and think about a time when you experienced the various positive and negative feelings. Write them down in your journal so you can remember them. For example, what are the times in your life circumstances that you were frightened, confused, sad, humiliated, disappointed, or threatened? What were the times that you were grateful, relieved, proud, or in love? When did you feel angry, delighted, disappointed, embarrassed, enraged, flawed, grieved, guilty, overwhelmed, in a state of panic, insignificant, regretful, surprised, scared, threatened, trapped, or worried?

Now practice using your list in real-life situations. For example, when you experience someone else behaving in a way that is difficult for you to understand, or is frustrating or unpleasant, search your emotional library to find similar feelings that help you see the world through their eyes.

Reversing Roles

Consider situations, issues, or topics about which you hold a strong opinion. These may be small situations that trigger anger, such as the way other people drive, fail to be on time, or do their work in a sloppy manner. Other examples may include political opinions, such as being "pro-life" or "pro-choice" regarding the abortion issue, thoughts about various political candidates, or opinions about food, spending, or even your favorite sports team.

First imagine that you're speaking with someone who holds the opposing view, or actually speak with someone who holds the opposing view. Now reverse roles for at least fifteen minutes and take the *opposite* opinion and perspective. As you take the opposite position, try to really see the world through the other person's eyes. What is the person with this perspective feeling? What are they thinking? Now try to think of a time in your life when you experienced similar feelings, even if the actual topic or situation was different. Afterward, write down some of the thoughts and emotions you experience in your journal as you assumed the other person's role. After fifteen minutes, you can return to seeing the world through your eyes. Do you see it any differently? Whether or not this exercise results in any changes in your own opinions, practicing this skill helps you to increase your ability to take another person's perspective, thus enhancing your ability to be empathetic and foster relationships.

Apply this Skill in Real Life

Whenever you find yourself engaged in any competitive, opposing, or angry thought toward others, first catch yourself and place your tendency to react on temporary hold for at least five minutes. Try listening carefully to what is the other person saying and what they're feeling (if you have difficulty doing this, you may want to review the instructions for how to listen effectively in chapter 6). Search for times in your emotional library when you may have experienced similar feelings. Use the experience to see the situation from the other person's perspective, and try to understand what they are feeling. Notice how you think about yourself afterward. Do you perceive yourself as more open-minded, more empathic, more considerate, or more wise? If so, reinforce your hard work and enjoy your new abilities. If not, continue to practice until you see results.

In the two tools we've just explained, we focused on methods to increase empathy in ways that are likely to result in the desire to increase compassionate action. With the following tool, we provide a way for you to increase the empathy you receive from others.

Seeking and Rewarding Empathy in Others

This last tool can be helpful to your relationships since you will build and reinforce empathic understanding in others. When you perceive that your own feelings are being shared or felt by another person, you experience a sense of being appreciated, valued, and respected. This leads to increased self-esteem.

When you have the opportunity, let others know how you feel. If they indicate that they understand what you're going through and you believe that they are sharing in your feelings, let them know and express your appreciation. For example, you may want to say, "I can tell that you're able to share this feeling with me. I really appreciate that—I know its not always easy to see the world through my eyes. It's helpful and comforting to me." If others do anything to help relieve your suffering in any way, be sure to let them know how they have been helpful.

If they do not indicate that they understand and you believe that their own reactions inhibit their ability to share your feelings, you might say, "What would be most helpful to me right now is to know that you are trying to share my feelings with me."

The last tool in this chapter underscores the fact that, although many people may want to help, they often simply don't know how to best support their friends or family members. It is designed to help you enhance relationships and focuses on how you can increase the help and support you need from the other people in your life.

Getting the Support You Need from Others

Since the earliest times in history, people who stood together and supported each other have had a better chance of survival, and this is as true today as it was then. This isn't only true for physical survival; it's important to psychological and emotional survival as well. Scientific studies have shown that there is a very strong link between social support and psychological, emotional, and physical well-being.

Social support usually refers to a positive relationship with another person. A positive relationship can be any relationship in which we experience pleasure, respect, understanding, help, companionship, or stimulation. The idea of social support can even be extended to animals or pets, which often provide companionship, a sense of being needed, and comfort. Although most people consider having support in their communities a common-sense good idea, there is actually substantial psychological and medical research showing that people who have good social support tend not only to be happier, but have a better overall quality-of-life and greater longevity. On the other hand, people who tend to be very isolated and distant from others often experience harmful effects on their life. These can include loneliness, mental and emotional problems, and a worsening of physical problems.

The following are some reasons that scientists have identified as to why social support is so important to your health.

“ People who know that others care often try to take better care of themselves. This can include doing things like maintaining good eating habits, exercising, and not smoking or drinking too much.

“ People who have someone to listen have a chance to "vent" and talk about bad experiences and negative feelings. When people don't have someone they trust to talk to, they sometimes try to block out emotions or may turn to drugs, alcohol, or other high-risk behaviors as a way of dealing with their problems.

❊ When receiving comfort, love, understanding, and care, people experience important biochemical and hormonal changes that may help their bodies (for example, their immune system) stay healthy.

❊ Other people can provide needed advice and guidance with problems. They can also help us reach our goals. They can be mentors, advisors, and colleagues.

It's also important to note that all social relationships are not good for your health. As you may have guessed, there is also a negative side to social connections. All the positive effects of social support are based upon getting the type of help you need from others, or what is called *positive social support*. We all know, for example, that a good marriage can contribute to good health, but a bad marriage can be very stressful and actually work against our health. All the reasons stated above have the reverse effect when the social connection is stressful, because the interaction with the other person is negative (for example, abusive, critical, angry, selfish, burdensome, frustrating). If a current relationship is negative, you may need to accept, change, or walk away from it. Many of the tools in this book may be of help. The tool you're about to learn is particularly useful for people who do not have their needed level of support from other people. This lack of support often results in people feeling sad, anxious, tense, or lonely.

Having positive social support serves to "protect" people from stress. Therefore, it's a good idea to try to develop a good social support system when you're doing okay, so when you need to call on friends during times of stress, they are there. The purpose of this tool is to help you to increase your positive social support. Don't wait for other people to make the first move. Your part in using this tool is to be creative in making sure that you get the social support you need. Here are some common obstacles that people come up against when trying to use this tool.

Common Questions and Answers about Social Support

Question: If I have to ask for it, is it still social support?

Our Answer: Of course. Some people think that you shouldn't have to ask another person for companionship, support, or to spend time together—that if they wanted to be with you, they would ask you. However, if you think about it, if everyone felt this way, no one would ever ask anybody!

Question: If I ask for support and get turned down, won't it make things worse?

Our Answer: No (that is, of course, unless you only focus on getting turned down and give up). Some people are afraid they'll be turned down if they invite someone out or suggest getting together. While this may be true, the odds are in your favor that you will probably get a positive response from most people. If two out of the next five people you attempt to get support from turn you down, that means that you will actually get the support from three of those five people. Even with the rejections, wouldn't you rather be receiving more support and companionship than you have right now?

Step 1: Make a List of People

Be creative when making this list and make sure that you include friends, neighbors, relatives, people from work or school, or people you encounter in your daily activities (like shopping, going to the dry cleaners, bank, or gas station), or members of the same community organizations (such as a charity, library, musical society, church, or political group).

Don't worry about any obstacles in the way, such as how busy they are, how far away they live, how well you know them, or how long since you've talked to them. Your first goal is have the longest list you can. Remember that telephone calls are often easier to arrange than inviting someone out. If there is someone you enjoy talking to on the phone, be sure to include them on the list.

Pets and animals are another kind of social support, so consider opportunities to spend more time with animals that you enjoy. For example, consider getting a pet, visiting someone with a pet you enjoy, going to the zoo, working at the animal shelter, volunteering at an animal clinic or veterinarian office, or visiting the aquarium.

Step 2: Make a Visit Plan

Decide how you will make your interaction pleasant for both of you. Think about the visit from the point of view of the other person as well as your own. Next to each name on your list, write down why you would like to see that person and also what they might enjoy about the visit with you. Here are some examples:

> ❧ "My friend Jane works for a computer software company. She would probably like giving me advice about software programs for learning a foreign language. I would enjoy getting a software program to learn French."

> ❧ "My brother is very busy and never gets time to cook anymore. I'll invite him over and get all the ingredients ready for his famous chili and ask him if he'd like to cook it with me for dinner."

> ❧ "The people from the church are always asking for help with the blood drive. If I help, I'll meet new people and feel needed, and the church will get free help."

Step 3: Increase Your Social Support

Now make plans to increase your social support by choosing at least one activity from your list to do this coming week. Identify a person, group, pet, or activity (for example, joining a bowling team or church choir) that represents an increase in your social support. For the next month, try to do at least one additional social event as a means of improving your positive social support.

Step 4: Make Your List Selective

Now go back over the list, this time looking for people who represent stress rather than a positive experience. For example, you may have a neighbor or relative who is always the center of attention and shows little concern for others. He is a person who is bound to disappoint you. Take such people off your list and politely refuse their invitations or visits. However, if you feel that a relationship is worth fighting for, then use additional tools in this chapter and throughout the book that focus on improving relationships.

Tracking Your Progress

You will know if your plans for companionship are successful by the number of times, either in person or on the telephone, that you are interacting with, enjoying, or being supported by other people (or animals) in your life.

Reward Yourself!

Your new sources of support are likely to be a strong reward in-and-of themselves. However, especially if you have had to overcome initial fears about being rejected or shyness about asking others to spend time together, you should be especially proud of yourself! Notice these changes and tell yourself that sometimes the risk is worth the outcome. Make attempts to increase your social support network each week for a month.

Enhancing relationships will continue to be an important part of your journey through LIFE and life. As you continue to practice the tools provided in this chapter, you may find that they are most helpful if combined with tools from other chapters.

CHAPTER 4

Fostering Acceptance

We cannot change anything unless we accept it.

—Carl Jung

Spirituality and Acceptance

Your spirituality can have a powerful effect on your ability to cope with the changes, pain, vulnerabilities, and losses that occur during life. Through the spiritual goal of acceptance, we come to view these aspects of life as inevitable and stop fighting for ways to avoid negative experiences. This doesn't mean we look for such experiences, but when they do happen, we are free to value both the positive and negative aspects of being alive and to increase our wisdom about ourselves, others, and the world around us. It is important to realize that our self-esteem is not enhanced by *what* happens to us, but h*ow we cope* with what happens to us. As such, this chapter is concerned with helping you to be more accepting of all that occurs in your life, both "good" *and* "bad."

Suffering Is Part of Life

Most of you are likely to be familiar with Helen Keller, a famous and courageous woman who was born multiply handicapped, lacking both sight and hearing, who was awarded the nation's highest civilian award, the Presidential Medal of Freedom. She is credited with the quote "Life is full of suffering—it is also full of overcoming it."

None of us are strangers to suffering, whether through transient problems such as temporary health concerns, interpersonal arguments, difficulty making changes, disappointments, or more profoundly painful incidents, such as the loss of a loved one, destructive family experiences, poverty, and chronic illness. All of us will certainly experience changes of circumstance, occasions of failure, and eventual death. Negative and distressful emotions are part of the human experience.

Despite the fact of suffering, many mental health, physical, and interpersonal difficulties are actually related to cycles of thoughts, feelings, and behavior that we use in an attempt to avoid, control, or change life's suffering. When we're not successful in these attempts, we can experience a loss of self-esteem. It's as if we expect ourselves to be able to avoid the pain, loss, and change that are a predictable and normal part of life. In addition, we frequently allow the experience of these negative emotions to block out positive experiences, working on the erroneous assumption that a range of both positive and negative experiences cannot exist at the same time.

A fundamental precept of Taoism, a centuries-old religion in China, is that ideas and concepts exist in pairs and that each part of the pair, while always opposite of the other, depends on the other for its own existence. A basic example is "good" and "evil." We only know good when we encounter it because we have known or encountered evil. Accepting this type of duality of our existence, the inevitable (and interdependent) presence of both positive and negative experiences in our lives, can also help us to be more at peace. According to Dr. Lin Yutang—"peace of mind is that mental condition in which you have accepted the worst." Acceptance brings peace because we appreciate and feel prepared for the full spectrum of life.

Your spirituality can serve as a powerful way to break free of the attempt to control and increase your ability to cope with life's inevitable suffering. For many people, their spirituality refers to a relationship with a power or force that transcends the everyday human experience yet is always present and accessible, even in times of change or suffering. Regardless of the actual spiritual truth or doctrine one believes, acceptance of the pain of the human experience and surrender to a "Higher Power" as a guiding force through difficult times is an important component of many spiritual philosophies. Giving up our need for control can also be viewed from a psychological perspective as giving up the part of ourselves that has tried unsuccessfully to avoid negative feelings or cope perfectly with life changes. From this perspective, relinquishing control can also mean engaging in a willingness to take a new viewpoint, accepting that difficult times are a part of day-to-day life.

Open your arms to change.

—The Dalai Lama

We have seen many patients enter therapy with the assumption that if they could just get *rid* of the bad feelings they are experiencing, then they would have a better and satisfying existence. Indeed, distressing thoughts, feelings, and memories are often the reason why people seek therapy. In addition, many also believe that their negative thinking and upsetting emotions are evidence of their own weaknesses, disease, laziness, or uniquely unfortunate circumstances. However, these beliefs are typically based upon rules or logic in the form of self-talk that people have unfortunately learned through parents, peers, and culture. What is needed in order to cope with life challenges and increase acceptance is a shift in attitude.

Shifting Toward Acceptance

A shift in attitude is needed in order to begin to accept the negative moments of your life, and to ultimately accept *you*. Think about your own attempts to control or avoid negative feelings. Perhaps such efforts have not worked or even made you feel worse, contributing to a low sense of self-esteem. This is not unusual—we have observed that at the point of coming into treatment, many patients want desperately to focus on trying be less depressed, more self-confident, less impulsive, or less anxious, as a way to get rid of negative or uncomfortable feelings and lead a more fulfilled life. Our patients are often surprised to learn that there are alternative ways to view their negative experiences, including acceptance.

Shifting your attitude to one of acceptance involves relinquishing control, or letting go of listening to what your mind has been saying to you, and then using your experience as a guide to help you stop trying to control everything and discover what to do next. Psychologist Steven Hayes and colleagues refer to this concept of realizing the unworkability or futility of past ways of thinking about our difficulties as "creative hopelessness" (1999). Based upon scientific principles, theory, and research regarding the way people learn, they pioneered a type of therapy they call Acceptance and Commitment Therapy. Through this approach, encouraging patients to be "creatively hopeless" means helping people to realize that their minds have been engaging in an ongoing, self-defeating, unworkable, and "hopeless" struggle to avoid any emotional distress. The important point is that *the struggle is in our own minds.* Taking a stance of creative hopelessness indicates that a person is willing to let go of this hopeless inner struggle and accept the presence of specific situations or negative feelings, even if they are not sure about what to do next.

The Tug-of-War

As an example, Dr. Hayes and his colleagues provide a "tug-of-war" metaphor. The idea of the tug-of-war came from a therapy patient at a point in his treatment where he was making the decision to let go of an internal struggle to control anxiety attacks. The patient described the situation as similar to being in a tug-of-war with a large and frightening monster, where both he and the monster are each grasping opposing ends of the rope over a huge, bottomless pit. The patient described himself on one end and the monster on the other, and despite his continued hard work, he felt like he was being pulled closer to the pit by the strong and powerful monster.

In an act of acceptance, this patient realized that he simply needed to drop the rope. The monster and pit are still there, but if the patient chose to no longer pull on the rope and engage in the struggle, there was a low likelihood that he would be pulled into the pit. We think that the important point of this story is that the patient doesn't have to win this game of tug-of-war! His mind has told him over and over that he must, but his experience is making him realize that this is not true.

Think about your own current struggles. Frequent struggles that we have heard from our patients (or experienced ourselves) over the years have included the belief that a "good" life is based upon being emotionally stronger, getting greater approval, controlling other people's reactions, achieving more power, having the most fun, gaining more recognition, or being taken care of. Inherent in so many of these struggles is a capital "C" for Control. Perhaps your own need for control keeps you from letting go (that is, dropping your own rope) and accepting your negative emotions as simply part of being human.

Acceptance and Self-Esteem

When we accept problems, distress, and painful emotions as being present in even the fullest, most satisfying life, we realize that self-esteem is not equal to a perfectly happy and pain-free existence. When you accept the inevitable and predictable painful or disappointing side of life, you are less likely to expend energy in trying to control everything that you experience. This provides you with a freedom to learn from challenges and make effective decisions about what is important to you and what to do next. As you allow and accept negative emotions to be part of your human experience, you become more willing to see how they can serve as a useful tool to better understand yourself and solve problems. As a result, fighting or avoiding negative feelings becomes less important to you and is replaced by the desire to take more responsibility for reducing life's suffering for yourself and others. Paradoxically, giving up an unrealistic desire to control the universe often leads to an increased sense of control over ourselves. This increased sense of control provides you with confidence to make choices and trust yourself, important ingredients for self-esteem.

Take the Plunge

One of the most popular temples in Japan, Kyomizu (Japanese for "clear water") Temple is located in Kyoto, and its main building stands on a large wooden terrace at the top of a hill. It was originally built as a Buddhist monastery in the year 798, and it's famous for its wooden terrace that provides dramatic views of the hillside, pathways, and foliage below. Having visited this temple ourselves, we can attest to the dramatic nature of the overall vista.

There is an expression in Japan that when someone is making an important or life-altering decision that they are metaphorically jumping off the Kyomizu terrace overlook. Standing at the site, with the sounds of the temple gong and trickling spring water as a backdrop, it's easy to imagine how such an expression evolved as many people looked out from the terrace, contemplating a life change. Are you ready to take such a leap of faith and make an important choice for greater self-acceptance? Are you willing to give up your unrealistic desire to control the universe and accept that negative emotions and experiences are not only a part of your life but a way to actually enlighten and enrich your spiritual journey? If so, the tools in this chapter can help!

Increasing Acceptance

The following tools are designed to help you practice greater self-acceptance, as well as acceptance of the inevitable changes, losses, and pains of life. Perhaps you have grown up with beliefs that support the idea that you must change any negative emotions that you or others experience. This sets up a vicious cycle of sacrificing yourself to try to make everyone else happy. The cycle can leave you feeling depressed, dissatisfied, resentful, and scared. The strategy outlined below is designed to help you accept the presence of negative emotions and increase your willingness to understand that they are an important part of being human.

Changing the Myths about Feeling Good

Psychologist Steven Hayes and his colleagues have identified several "myths" or beliefs that represent the type of self-instruction that people commonly learn as rules to guide them through difficult psychological or emotional moments. The following tool is adapted from their list of myths that involve an unrealistic set of standards to which we can never adhere, no matter how hard we try (Hayes, Strosahl, and Wilson 1999, 145). We have expectations of meeting these standards and feel like failures when we can't.

By using the following list, you can identify the specific myths that you find yourself trying to live up to when you have a painful thought, feeling, or memory. You then can make an important step toward stopping your internal struggle and accepting these experiences as a normal part of life.

Step 1: Consider the Myth

The list below contains common myths which are followed by the actual facts that contradict the myth. Read each myth, and then try to think of an experience from you own life in which you try to "live up to" the myth. Don't be concerned if you can't think of an example from your own life for every myth. Some people are more prone to believe one type of myth than others, based upon their upbringing or learning history.

Step 2: Contradict the Myth

After you consider each myth, read carefully the facts that contradict the myth and use your own experience to confirm these facts. Now make a commitment to be willing to *drop* this myth and rely on the actual facts about feelings the next time you're in an emotionally difficult situation.

Step 3: Remind Yourself

Finally, we suggest that you post a list of the myths that most apply to you on your refrigerator or mirror, or else carry a small list in your wallet or purse to remind yourself to accept the facts and stop reacting as if the myths were true.

Common Myths

❧ *Myth 1:* Negative thoughts, feelings, and memories will hurt you if you don't do something to immediately get rid of them.

❧ *Actual Facts:* This is not true. Experiencing negative thoughts, feelings, and memories means that you are human. They can be very useful in helping you notice things about your life that are meaningful to you or that need to change. When negative experiences occur, you will naturally be hurting. It makes sense to care for yourself and try your best to manage your feelings so that you understand why you're hurting. Feelings, by their very nature, change with circumstances and the way you are looking at the world. They do not cause any lasting physical damage.

❧ *Myth 2:* Understanding why I have negative feelings will make them go away.

❧ *Actual Facts:* Although it is certainly helpful to understand why you're experiencing negative feelings, it's unrealistic to expect that you can eliminate them simply by understanding them. For example, if you are very sad because you have experienced a loss, it's easy to see that understanding the root of your sadness does not make it go away. In fact, putting your energy toward controlling this sadness will only make it worse. Instead, work to accept challenging feelings, be mindful of them, let them happen, and let them pass. You may wish to practice the mindfulness meditation exercises you learned in chapter 2 to help ride them out. One basic Buddhist tenet that is very applicable here suggests that it is far less important to understand how our suffering came about than to do what we can in the present to end it.

❧ *Myth 3:* Being mentally healthy means that I can control and eliminate negative feelings.

❧ *Actual Facts:* Being mentally healthy actually means being able to notice and manage negative feelings without the need to rationalize and judge them. They are more likely to pass if you don't spend significant time trying to justify their existence or getting down on yourself for having them. Justifying usually involves some type of blame, and you do not ever have to blame someone else for your feelings. They are yours, they are present, and it serves you to accept them—*period.*

❧ *Myth 4:* Being emotionally healthy means being happy.

❧ *Actual Facts:* It's a very common mistake to believe in the myth that emotionally healthy people are always happy. Being healthy means being okay with who you are and accepting that you will experience a wide range of emotions. Being able to admit that you're not always happy and are learning to accept negative moments represents a true path to happiness and peace.

❧ *Myth 5:* The inability to control a negative reaction is a sign of weakness or ignorance.

❧ *Actual Facts:* The need to try to control feelings is actually a sign that a problem exists. Negative emotional experiences are an important part of being human, and your emotions can make you aware of what is truly important to you. Denying your feelings is like trying to deny who you are. Feelings are never the problem. What people do to control or avoid these feelings, or certain ways they choose to behave in response to their feelings, can create additional problems.

❧ *Myth 6:* Manifestations of negative feelings such as crying, sadness, fatigue, and confusion, are clear signs of personality problems.

❧ *Actual Facts:* When negative emotions are intense, it is common to experience tearfulness, crying, fatigue, and confusion. After all, you are probably very focused on managing your challenging emotions, and concentration may be difficult. Expressing difficult feelings can also create an energy drain and result in feelings of fatigue. Author Marianne

Williamson (2002) tells a story about an old Buddhist monk who stood crying at the grave of a mentor. When a curious passerby asked, "Why do you cry? I thought you were enlightened." The monk simply replied, "Because I am sad." When people accept that negative emotions are an inevitable part of being alive and are willing to tolerate such feelings in others, this is personality *strength* rather than a personality *weakness*.

❊ *Myth 7:* People who are in control of their lives are generally able to control how they react and feel.

❊ *Actual Facts:* People who are in control of their lives may be in control of their behavior, but rarely need to try to control their reactions or feelings. Many people may confuse being in control of behavior with being in control of feelings. However, this is an important distinction. For example, if you are being treated unfairly, it's important not to ignore your feelings of sadness, disappointment, or anger. How you choose to act on those feelings, however, is in your control.

Looking over these myths and actual facts daily will help you to practice accepting your own feelings by keeping aware of those myths that you may need to unlearn. Now we move on to strategies that focus on acceptance of events that are outside yourself.

> When I have a toothache, I discover that not having a toothache is a wonderful thing. That is peace.
> —Thich Nhat Hanh

Accepting Negative Events, Change, & Loss

Although we all know that life can be cruel, many of us continue to hold onto the unrealistic expectation that we will not have to suffer. Where did we get such expectations? We all know of generous and caring souls who experience terrible and painful events. We know of these instances through personal friends, family members, celebrities, and historical figures. We know of entire populations that have been enslaved, tortured, or disregarded. We know that for every one of us, death is a certainty. Perhaps because we know this, we use our sophisticated reasoning in an attempt to control what we know is inevitable. For example, we try to reduce our chances of personal injury, we watch the news for information concerning the best diets or drugs to keep us from developing illness, and many people view the bad events and suffering of the world as a message, judgment, or punishment by a Higher Power. However, such reactions are often nothing more than minds trying to get some illusory control over the future.

Negative Events Can Move You Forward

After knowing many people through our own personal life situations, our psychotherapy practice, and our clinical research with mental and physical illness, we have come to believe strongly that negative events in and of themselves do not interrupt or block people's spiritual journeys. They do bring home to most of us the fragile nature of health, power, or any tangible success we experience. They also can help us move forward in our spiritual journey and increasing our self-esteem.

You're probably thinking "I intellectually understand that bad things happen, that such things are an inevitable part of life, and that I can even learn from such experiences. But how do I accept the bad things that are happening in my life *right now?*" Our answer is that you start right now, but you learn it gradually. By committing yourself to the goal of acceptance and using the following tool, to work toward gaining acceptance, you will be more likely to keep trying rather than expect it to happen all at once. Note that we provide more in-depth training on how to solve day-to-day problems in chapter 9.

Practicing Acceptance of Negative Events, Change, & Loss

This useful tool is based on our research on problem solving, and will help you cope with challenges as they arise in everyday life.

Step 1: List Difficulties

Write down the event that you're having difficulty accepting. As an example, one of our patients, Mike, wrote down, "My friend Paul was diagnosed with leukemia."

Step 2: Determine Where the Problem Lies

Write down what part of this event that makes it difficult for you to accept. You need to be very honest here and write down what *truly* makes it difficult. Even if you find yourself criticizing your own thoughts with self-statements such as "I sound selfish, afraid, or shallow." For the example above, Mike wrote down, "Paul's too young—how could God let this happen to a sweetheart of a guy like Paul? I think about how much fun we have and how we will not be able to have fun traveling together for a long time—maybe never. Paul and I both love bike riding and used to travel all over the world on our bike trips. I try to avoid thinking about it because it makes me too upset."

Step 3: List the Consequences

Write down what you view as the consequences of accepting this event. What are the choices that you could make now to help you become more accepting? Regarding the example above, Mike responded, "I can be with him (but it's difficult for me to do that without crying, and I feel stupid crying). I can give up traveling for a few months (I am disappointed, as we had a trip planned to Europe this summer). I can probably find other ways to enjoy my love for travel. I could travel alone or with others and ask Paul's help (but I feel guilty because my friend may feel bad)."

Step 4: Choose What You Can Change

From the information you wrote down in step 3, choose *one* thing you can change in yourself to help you adjust to the event. Write down a plan for how you'll commit yourself to making this change to help you accept what is happening. Mike's situation provides an excellent example of how much acceptance means being willing to change something in ourselves. For example, if Mike were to change any of his reported thoughts (indicated in the parentheses), he would be better able to accept this event. These include any of the following:

- Being willing to show his emotions to his friend. Please note that we realize that this is uncomfortable for Mike. We suggest that he can be willing even though he realizes that this may cause him to feel uncomfortable.

- Being open to experiencing disappointment regarding the cancellation of his trip.

- Considering other options to satisfy his love of travel.

Step 5: Choose One Thing

Now think about what you can specifically do to reduce suffering for yourself and others in this situation. This may include items from the list you just made, or you may add new ideas as you think about reducing suffering in others. In Mike's case, allowing himself to be angry at God was particularly difficult. He struggled with thoughts that God was unfair versus fear that he was wrong to question God. When these conflicts arose, he was tempted to give up, but his commitment to try to tolerate his negative feelings kept him on track. He later reported that this struggle made him realize how he never thought about unfairness when he received something good that he didn't especially deserve, for example, his own health. How often do any of us also experience this lopsided philosophy of fairness?

Mike chose to try to share his emotions with his friend Paul. Like most things of which we are afraid, it became easier for him to do once he started. Mike additionally worked toward reducing his own guilt about being sad that he canceled the trip to help Paul through his cancer treatment. To do this, he made a list of statements he could say to himself that countered guilt and embarrassment about his feelings of sadness (for example, "I can be sad about missing the trip and still be glad I am here to support my friend."), choosing to let the feelings be present but not allow them to get in the way of the things he needed to do. He also visited Paul often and as an alternative to traveling together, rented travel videos, made a scrapbook of their trips together and listed places that they would like to visit in the future.

Step 6: Pick Yourself Up

Be willing to get up again! When people experience difficulty with acceptance, they often say that it's just too difficult to do and that they doubt that they will ever be able to accept certain negative events. It's almost as if they are saying that in order to accept something, we must agree with it and experience no negative feelings. This is an impossible task—no wonder so many people give up. Acceptance means that you tolerate your negative feelings and are willing to see suffering as part of life, and maybe even a factor that allows you to value your other experiences more intensely.

When did you ever succeed 100 percent the first time you attempted a difficult task? Transforming your fears of suffering into acceptance of suffering is one of the most difficult lessons to learn. As you try to do this, reflect on the other difficult lessons you learned throughout your life. Remember all the scraped knees you endured as you learned to ride a bike or roller-skate? Perhaps you can think of all your initial attempts to cook a meal, write a term paper, sing a song, or work out at the gym. For both of us, it took a combined total of seven attempts (some partially successful) over our lifetimes before we were able to transform ourselves into non-smokers. We had to know that the final result was important, using experience with failures to learn about the pitfalls of trying to change, and we had to commit to the change process. Transforming yourself toward acceptance means that when you fall short of perfect acceptance, you get up, brush off the dirt, get back on your feet, and try once again. Like all important lessons, the effort will be worth it. It is worthwhile to repeat a quote here by Confucius that we first introduced in chapter 1, "Our greatest glory is not in never falling, but in rising every time we fall."

Fostering Gratitude as a Form of Acceptance

Accepting negative events as a part of life, and learning to view them as opportunities to learn, is very important to our self-esteem. Creating such learning opportunities can really boost self-confidence. However, there are also many times we have difficulty facing situations that are not true instances of pain, loss, or suffering. For example, times that you experience resentment, envy, bitterness, or disappointment over the things you don't have or the things you want more of. Such things may include money, popularity, leisure time, clothes, good looks, intelligence, and achievements, to name a few. We're not saying that there is something inherently bad or destructive about wealth, achievement, or admiration, but there is something very destructive about emotionally focusing yourself on what you don't have or what others have. This only hurts your ability to awaken your self-esteem.

The next tool that we provide is designed to help you increase your joy, wonder, and thankfulness for what you have—in other words, your sense of gratitude. In learning to use this tool, remember the words of Anne Frank, "Think of all the beauty still left around you and be happy."

Increasing our gratitude is a way of keeping an awareness or focus on accepting what we have been given. Gratitude has been described as a sense of joyful surprise, wonder, and appreciation for life. Psychologist Michael McCullough (2002), who studies gratitude, has described it as our tendency to recognize and respond with positive emotion to other people's caring actions, the positive experiences we encounter, and the good outcomes we obtain. Whatever your definition, we know that gratitude is often associated with spirituality, positive emotions, and an increased sense of well-being. One reason for this heightened sense of well-being is that grateful people see themselves as the recipient of others' caring or generosity. As such, they are likely to have experiences of increased self-affirmation or self-value, greater social support, and improved self-esteem.

How Do You React to Gifts?

When you receive a surprise gift or experience an unexpected positive outcome in your life, how do you react? Perhaps you are pleased and appreciative. At other times, you may be uncomfortable. Here are a few examples of reported difficulty that some people report when they are faced with either unexpected gifts or good outcomes in their lives. One patient, Jill, complained that coming from a wealthy family may have seemed advantageous to others, but her self-esteem was always fragile because she saw herself as spoiled and getting things free without earning them. Another patient, Carl, was fearful of Christmas, birthdays, and other gift-giving holidays because he anticipated having his gifts judged by the receiver and compared the gifts he was getting in return. Alice didn't want to invite a new friend to her wedding because she felt uncomfortable having this new friend think that she expected a gift. Fran, the mother of five grown children, would lament that each of her children liked the presents they received from each other more than the ones they received from her.

All of these reactions are examples of our need to see ourselves as worthy. We want to be sure that we have done enough to deserve others' gifts to us and to erase any chance of anxiety or self-doubt concerning the whole gift-giving process. Here is a chance for you to accept a little anxiety in your life. Particularly when it may only mean that you're experiencing some discomfort with the idea that you did nothing in particular to earn, deserve, or have a right to the gift. If you give into or fuel these thoughts, your self-esteem can suffer. An alternative, more productive view is to conclude that whether or not you are "worthy" of the gift is unimportant. What *is* important to your own mental and physical health, as well as your actions toward others, is that you recognize the gift, accept the gift, and allow yourself to be thankful for the gift.

Think about the last time you gave a gift for the sole purpose of increasing that person's happiness. Which reaction would you have preferred to witness in your recipient—anxiety and worry over their worthiness to get the gift or recognition, acceptance, delight, and gratitude? We ask you to consider the following scenario in order to stimulate your thinking about gratitude and recognize where you might need to work on your ability to experience it. Although this exercise is simply designed to make you think, you may want to write down your responses in your journal. Writing often helps the thinking process.

Practicing Gratitude

Imagine that you have received an unexpected gift from a distant cousin. You answer your doorbell and discover that you've been sent something that you want, can use, or really admire. There is a card that says, "I know that this is something that will bring you joy—I care about you and want you to be happy." What is your reaction?

As you consider or write down what your own reaction might be, some of the answers we have received from others are provided below with a brief commentary about what we believe is "behind" each statement.

What does he want of me? Answers such as this reveal a suspicion that if anyone would do something nice for you, they must have an ulterior motive other than your happiness. This response contains a strong element of fear that you're expected to do something in return but also involves anxiety and confusion over what you are supposed to do.

What did I do to deserve this? Answers such as this reveal a disbelief in your worth or value to the extent that anyone would be motivated to provide a gift with the sole intention of increasing your happiness. As a result, the response generally sparks a search for some evidence that, despite the recipient's unworthiness, they've done something specifically worthy of getting the gift.

What should I do with this? This response shows a confusion and lack of knowledge about what to do with a novel situation. The question about what to do with the gift is actually more accurately, "What do I do with this confusing and new feeling?" Also included in this type of response is, "If I send it back, will they be upset?" In this case, such people are already searching for ways to reduce their discomfort. What they don't realize is that taking away the distress in the moment can deprive them of the opportunity to understand themselves better and increase their self-acceptance, which will further help them to accept someone else's love. In other words, *you don't have to earn every good thing that happens to you.*

Why It's Important

With a little help and guidance, you will come to be more aware of the many surprise gifts that you receive "free of charge" in life. If you give into the tendency or urge to react to them with doubts and fear, you cut off an important opportunity to continue on your path to self-esteem. The interesting thing is that when you allow yourself to accept gifts, you find yourself being grateful not only for the gift itself, but the energy and attention to the gift that was extended by the giver. By allowing yourself to be worthy, you often want to share the feeling and give to others—not in order to return the gift, but to bring joy to someone who is not expecting anything from you.

Getting back to everyday life situations, let's look at some of the gifts you may have received, but which you ignored or were not grateful for *over the past week.* We'll start you off by pointing out common gifts that people receive. You may want to jot down in your journal some of these free gifts that you've received so you can remember to practice being grateful in the future. However, please don't stop with these. Go ahead and add to your own inventory of free gifts on which you can focus your gratitude.

Free Gifts

❄ *The gift of healing.* Remember the miracle that occurred when the paper cut on your finger disappeared after a few days? Consider for a moment the complicated array of biological and physiological "miracles" that occur every day to heal wounds, adapt your body to environmental changes, pump blood through you body to nourish vital organs, and battle invading cancer cells? Have you let these gifts of healing go unrecognized?

❄ *The gift of paid employment.* Despite the turmoil, problems, daily hassles, and stress of your work, consider the millions of people in the world who have no means of gainful employment. In addition, consider all the work you do, such as house cleaning, laundry, personal accounting, and walking the dog, for which you don't get paid. This doesn't mean that you ignore problems with your work—just that your gratitude for the gift of employment will help to keep your emotions positive and manage the day-to-day stressors that you face.

❧ *The gifts of other people.* Think about the people in your life now who have turned out to be wonderful and surprising gifts. You did not actively seek them out or pursue them. Nevertheless, their friendship has happened in your life. They provide you with gifts of support and caring simply because they want to share life with you. What miracles these people are!

❧ *The gifts of nourishment, transportation, or educational experiences.* Imagine the possibilities for gratitude if you stop to notice the gifts you have that enable you to have access to clean water or healthy food. Have you recognized the gift of someone who cooks meals for you or your own ability to cook a meal? Think about the gifts you have available to be able to drive a car, fly thousands of miles in just hours on an airplane, or ride in an air-conditioned bus. We have all been ungrateful at times for our educational opportunities, focusing on unfair teachers, crowded classrooms, too much homework, or having to get up too early. Imagine how our emotions would shift during day-to-day experiences if we were more grateful for the chance to learn something new every day.

As we indicated, gratitude often results in the desire to share gifts with others. Below are two brief, but profound, moments of gratitude that each of us have recorded in our own memories.

Art's Personal Account of Gratitude

On a recent trip to Japan, we visited the Nezu Jinja (jinja is Japanese for "shrine") in Tokyo as part of a birthday celebration for Art. The celebration included Shinto purification, offerings, prayer, and traditional birthday gifts from the shrine's Shinto priest. There is great reverence and significance to such celebrations, which have existed for centuries in Japan. As one who is usually more comfortable in giving rather than receiving gifts, Art approached the celebration with a degree of discomfort, sensing that he would have the unfamiliar role as the center of attention and receiver of gifts. In other words, how could he be sure that he "deserved" such attention? At the end of the ceremony, however, his experience was one of profound gratitude. Concern and discomfort seemed insignificant compared to the joy he experienced in recognition of a few merged "spirits" in a special place, at a moment in time, for the sole purpose of giving him joy.

> And be content with such things as ye have.
>
> —Bible (Hebrews)

Christine's Personal Account of Gratitude

For Christine, moments of profound gratitude are experienced during church services. Although there may be many other places that stimulate her spirituality and gratitude, such as the view of a beach at dawn or the faces of her husband and children, this experience represents one unexpected gift that she has received through no effort or specific intention on her part. Specifically, during various moments of the service, there is an opportunity to experience the shared love of the many different people gathered together at one time, in one place, in a moment of joyful interaction. In the urban church we attend, there is a remarkable diversity of people—young, old, many different ethnic, cultural, intellectual and educational backgrounds, gay and heterosexual, people challenged with mental, physical, or addictive disabilities, and those celebrating good health. The insight provided by a service at this church, for Christine, is truly a gift. It is similar to that experienced by a child seeing Disneyland for the first time—a magic kingdom where every soul is precious, valuable, and connected.

Reap the Rewards

Gratitude focuses on the gift we have been given and it is virtually impossible to experience worry, anger, greed, or victimization at the same moment that you experience a strong sense of gratitude. In addition, studies have shown that gratitude increases our well-being by replacing resentment, regret, and other negative psychological states with the experience of happiness, optimism, hope, and life satisfaction.

In psychology, researchers have spent much time and energy developing ways to reduce negative emotions and self-destructive thought patterns. Recently, however, many of us have begun to focus very serious attention on the profound effects of positive emotions, like gratitude, in our lives.

As many gratitude researchers have discovered, this emotion inspires the intention to share gifts with others. For us both, gratitude is a reason for writing this book.

How to Do It

Take out your journal now and use the following instructions for increasing your gratitude for the large and small gifts in your life that you receive from others, through natural forces, or from the source of your own spiritual faith.

Step 1: List Two Things

Write in your journal for the next two weeks. Each day, write down at least two things for which you were grateful during that day. The way to identify the things for which you're grateful is to be on the lookout for even small moments in which you experienced a surge of joy. If you find it difficult to limit yourself to two things, great! Don't feel that you have to stop at two. Remember that anything can qualify. For example, our own personal lists have included things as big as the support and love we give to each other, a chance to share various moments with our children, or being able to help our patients, as well as small things, such as the chance to hear a great CD, take a hot shower, taste good wine, feel the sun's warmth on our faces, or take a walk.

Step 2: Review Your List

At the end of the second week, read over all of the things that you wrote down. Notice how, at the moment you re-experience your gratitude, there is an absence of envy, jealously, or material desire.

Step 3: Use Your Gratitude

When you're experiencing feelings of envy, anger, jealousy, or just plain self-pity, take out your list and review all the things you are grateful for. Allow yourself to focus on any one pleasant gift. Close your eyes, breathe deeply, and allow gratitude to fill your heart. Remember the ancient Persian saying, "I wept because I had no shoes, until I saw a man who had no feet."

Making Mistakes

We now turn to the final tool in this chapter, a technique that is also focused on the goal of acceptance. This strategy extends the idea of gratitude for life's gifts to include even recognizing, accepting, and being grateful for our mistakes.

As a human being, you have a natural tendency to learn (you are learning all of the time, but just don't always realize it). When you make a mistake you probably, like most of us, regret it at first. But when you reconsider and see this mistake with the view of teaching yourself something new, you can enhance your confidence and increase your self-esteem. We're betting that some of the greatest learning experiences of your life probably came from mistakes that you made. At the time, you probably didn't think to yourself, "Oh boy, I'm sure glad I experienced this difficulty and made this mistake." The learning experience came later, when you found yourself telling someone what you learned from the experience.

Your Research Project on Mistakes

The following research project is similar to one you may have completed when you were in high school, where you researched a topic and came up with some conclusions, suggestions, or opinions about the topic. We have designed this project to help you become more of an expert about making mistakes. You will need to have your journal handy once again.

Step 1: Check It Out

Research the topic. Find out how common mistakes are for the people around you. Ask anyone you know, "Did you ever make a mistake? What did you learn from it?" You may feel a bit silly asking at first, but remember that you're on a mission to learn.

Step 2: Decide How You Feel

Write down how you generally feel about the mistakes people make and why people make mistakes (for example, they're not paying attention or thinking carefully, they are unsure of facts or information, they're trying to be helpful but may not know what to do, they didn't care enough about a specific situation, they can be clumsy or unskilled, or that it's simply part of being human).

Step 3: List Your Own

List your own history of mistakes, from small mishaps to great hazards. This doesn't have to be an exhaustive list—just what springs to mind in the next five minutes or so. Make a column of the things you learned and the "terrible" consequences of your mistake. Now see which column has more in it.

Step 4: Accept Them

Embrace your mistakes! Only you can make the mistakes that you've made in your life situations. That makes your mistakes unique (although many other people have probably made similar mistakes). Write down your favorite mistakes and favorite lessons learned.

Step 5: Share Them

Be on the lookout for ways in which you can share the mistakes and the lessons you have learned with others, particularly when they seem to be looking for your guidance and reassurance. You may choose to share your mistakes with your children, coworkers, friends, or students. Ask them if hearing about your mistakes and subsequent lessons was helpful.

Step 6: Find New Ones

Search for mistakes! Look at each new mistake as the gift or a new lesson to learn. Consider yourself fortunate, like someone finding a four-leaf clover, the next time you make a mistake. Think of it as a chance to learn more, grow wiser, and not have to pay tuition costs.

Remember, as the ancient Chinese philosopher and founder of Taoism, Lao-tze, once stated, "Failure is the foundation of success, and the means by which it is achieved."

Learning acceptance often involves a sustained effort to recognize and remember the futility of trying to control all painful situations. You have the choice to give up this struggle and accept that neither you nor your life situations are perfect. There is no need to avoid moments of fear, failure, or sadness. These experiences are part of everyone's life.

CHAPTER 5

Learning Forgiveness

Blessed are the merciful, for they obtain mercy.

—Mathew 5:7

The Challenge of Forgiveness

Many spiritual leaders and counselors have observed that people's experience of anger and the inability to forgive others or themselves serve as major obstacles to their spiritual advancement. Many of us fear that the act of forgiveness will be actually viewed as an act of weakness or lack of self-respect, and a vicious cycle ensues to interrupt our sense of peace. The truth is that when we successfully learn to forgive, we actually free ourselves to move on with our lives. As a result, our self-esteem and sense of well-being are strengthened. As Buddha suggested centuries ago, "Those who are free of resentful thoughts surely find peace." As such, the tools in this chapter are provided to help you with the hard work involved in learning to forgive.

Are You Struggling with Forgiveness?

You may currently be experiencing difficulty in forgiving yourself or others. If this is the case, learning how to forgive can be a daunting and challenging aspect of your spiritual journey. You may have a desire for justice—believing that the person or group of people that disappointed, hurt, or injured you in some way must "pay" or suffer for what they've done. If they suffer, your mind reasons, then it will be clear who was at fault, how badly you were hurt, and how much pain you experienced. You reason that your own suffering will lessen because it will be clear that the pain was caused by someone or something else and that you are only an innocent victim of your mental or emotional damage. The problem is that it's really not very helpful to you to make yourself a victim. But why do you feel the need to convince others that your suffering isn't your fault, especially when those who care about you probably don't need convincing? In fact, the reason you may work so hard to convince others is that you may really be trying to convince *yourself* of your innocence.

When you're having trouble letting go of anger, your difficulty may partially depend upon what your own internal critic is saying, such as, "He's the one who started it," "They don't care about me," or "She lied to me." Although it may be quite true that someone started an argument with you, treated you unfairly, or betrayed you in some way, there is a philosophy inherent in teachings as diverse and ancient as Buddhism, the Kabbala, and Christianity that your contact with every other person with whom you meet, including those you may consider "enemies" in your present, day-to-day world, can assist you in some way along in your spiritual journey. Consider the teachings of Rabbi Michael Berg (2001), one of the spiritual teachers of the Kabbala, who explains that the negative and destructive emotions we often experience toward other people don't originate with either them or us, but represent barriers that are placed in the way of spiritual transformation—barriers that can be removed with a little guidance and some hard work.

Three Common Forgiveness Situations

In our experience, there appears to be three instances in which we usually want to forgive, but find ourselves getting stuck and unable to meet the challenge of forgiveness. Let's take a look at each of them.

Forgiveness Fear

In the first case, an individual is asking for forgiveness, but you find it very difficult to meet this request. You realize that they may be sorry, but you have been hurt or let down, often repeatedly, and you're fearful to trust their apology and promise of change. You have told yourself that by forgiving them, you must instantly be able to trust them again. In this case, your own fear is the major barrier to your ability to forgive.

Forgiving an Unrepentant Person

In the second situation, people who you have difficulty forgiving are not remorseful and may not even believe they have done anything wrong. In fact, they may even think that you're the one at fault. In this case, you may feel trapped and crippled by the anger and sense of injustice you experience in response to their selfishness and egotistical attitude. You may believe that it's important to convince the other person that they have done something wrong and have them understand the pain they have "caused." The barrier to forgiveness here is a sense of moral outrage that will not budge because to remove the outrage is viewed by you as an admittance that the person did nothing wrong. Your sense of justice prevails.

This moral outrage isn't necessary. Letting go of anger does not excuse the hurt or loss created by the other person. As forgiveness researchers and psychologist Robert Enright and colleagues (2000; 2001) have pointed out, forgiveness is not the same as pardon, condoning, or even reconciliation. You can forgive and at the same time decide that you do not wish to spend time or work at building a more trusting relationship with people who are so reluctant to take responsibility for their actions.

Forgiving Yourself

In a third forgiveness situation, you are concerned that you have some done something wrong yourself, but angry thoughts often allow you to keep the blame on others and away from you. In this case, putting your attention on the struggle to forgive the other person is a big distraction from the needed task of looking to yourself and facing your own thoughts of guilt or self-criticism. Self-criticism can actually be very useful and helpful on your spiritual journey—as long as it is constructive.

All cases in which you're experiencing difficulty in forgiving can be points for choice in your life, opportunities to move yourself

forward on your journey or stay back and place your emotional energies on a past event—a past that can't be changed. Forgiveness (of
yourself or others) is a gift you give yourself—to remove the suffering that is standing in the way of your moving forward toward
greater self-esteem and well-being. As Harriet Nelson suggested,
"Forgive all who have offended you, not for them, but for yourself."

Tools for Learning Forgiveness

The tools used in this chapter are designed to help you learn how to
forgive and to increase your understanding that an inability to
forgive is far more harmful to you than the person who has injured,
insulted, or harmed you in some way. If you would like to learn how
to increase your ability to forgive, these tools may be helpful to you.

The first tool is adapted from strategies and principles from
both cognitive therapy (for example, Beck 1993), as well as rational-
emotive therapy, the latter being pioneered by psychologist Albert
Ellis (2001). It teaches you to change the statements about forgiveness that you have learned to say to yourself. In other chapters, we
presented ways to change the thoughts or rules that our minds have
learned to say over our lifetime. In this chapter, we spend some time
helping you to change inaccurate thoughts that specifically block
your ability to forgive. To introduce the first tool, which focuses on
changing unforgiving thoughts, we describe one of our patients, Bob.

Bob's Challenge with Forgiveness

Bob had not seen his brother in two years. The older of two
sons, he was frequently called upon as he was growing up to care for
his brother Jim, seven years his junior. As both grew older, they
grew apart. Their parents frequently compared Jim to his older
brother Bob, and as a result, Jim became bitter and jealous of anything good that happened in Bob's life. Jim seemed to resent Bob's
good fortune, for example, his marriage, teaching awards, and
friends. Bob was hurt that Jim's jealousy led him to avoid Bob and
ignore his attempts to call, send holiday cards, or invitations to his
home. Others often told Bob that his brother frequently put him
down. Bob was angry that Jim had chosen a path that was so
destructive to their relationship, and Jim didn't respond to any of
Bob's attempts to get together and talk about their problems. When
their father retired, both Jim and Bob were invited to the celebration.
Bob dreaded seeing his brother and knew that he would be better
able to enjoy the celebration if he was able to forgive Jim, but Jim did

not want to be forgiven—he didn't think he'd done anything wrong. The logic of Bob's thinking was as follows:

1. "I have been successful with my life, and Jim hates me for it."

2. "How dare he resent my happiness? I was always happy for him."

3. "Brothers should support each other, if they love each other. He must not love me."

4. "How can I forgive him if he doesn't even think he did anything wrong? This is too hard."

Bob's logic initially appears to accurately describe the situation. But as we look at the statements he's making to himself, notice that Bob has interpreted all of his brother's behavior as actions directly expressed toward him. This is called *personalization,* because when we engage in this type of thinking, we make ourselves the center of the universe with everyone's actions focused on *us* in some way. The way to catch ourselves in making this type of thinking error with regard to forgiveness is to become more aware of these common inaccuracies that come into our minds when we are experiencing difficulty letting go of anger. Let's take a few moments to identify such errors in thinking so you can practice changing them. Here are five common thinking errors that are often part of our unforgiving thoughts. After we describe these errors, we will return to Bob's story.

The Personalization Error

Two types of personalization errors occur with unforgiving thoughts. The first type involves a tendency to see the motivation for another person's actions in terms of the consequences for yourself. For example, if you're bullied, you see the bully's aggression as an attack on your weakness (as opposed to an example of their poor self-control). If someone challenges your argument, you see it as their attempt to make you look foolish rather than their curiosity or attempt to make their own opinion heard. This heightens your emotional reaction, as you see the other person's behavior as always directed toward you instead of considering the wide range of explanations for the behavior, many of which have little to do with you.

A second type of personalization is concerned with comparisons you make between yourself and the other person. You often find yourself making statements such as, "I would never do that" or "That's a wrong way to look at the situation." This makes you the arbiter of what people should and should not do—a kind of judge who everyone must come and stand before in order to determine if their behavior is within your "laws." In either type of personalization, the way to change your unforgiving thoughts is to change the focus of your thinking away from the other person and on *your own reactions.*

The Magnification Error

When you look at objects through a magnifying glass, they appear much larger than they really are. This thinking error occurs when we emphasize a statement, act, or situation to a point where it's way out of proportion with its actual importance. Small comments can become reasons for heightened anger and an inability to forgive. Insensitive acts can become assaults, making it much more difficult to forgive because our desired sense of justice must prevail. The more that we can magnify the person's error, the more we are justified in not forgiving.

The opposite view is one in which we minimize the *positive* aspects of someone else's behavior as a way of maintaining our unforgiving thoughts. For example, when someone who has acted hurtfully in the past engages now in a helpful or nurturing act, we may find ourselves minimizing or discounting it. In either situation, we feel justified in our desire to remain angry. We assume that if we remain angry, we will hurt less. Actually, such thinking only serves to further blanket us in toxic emotions. The logic that we often use to justify our tight grip on unforgiveness is that holding onto fear somehow feels safer than letting it go and possibly getting hurt again. The truth is that anger is far more harmful to our health and destructive to spiritual advancement than getting hurt.

The "Should" Error

This common thinking error includes all the rigid and inflexible rules that we have adopted over the years. Some of them are "if/then" statements that we have learned from our families, (for instance, "If I work hard, everyone should appreciate it and think well of me") and some are a combination of shared social rules mixed in with our own learning experience. Although you may use some of these rules positively, people often make thinking errors in which the rules, although sometimes accurate, become inflexible and indisputable. We see any deviation from the rules that we've learned as "bad" and start to perceive other people's actions as intolerable, incorrect, and unacceptable. What are actually differences of opinion, habit, or style become instances of law breaking that must be punished. For example, suppose that a person happens to bump into you on a movie line. They "should" watch where they are going, or they "should" apologize immediately, are instant reactive "shoulds" that people often assume before they actually get the facts of what has just happened. Most people would agree that these shoulds are appropriate social responses to what has happened. For example, if this were to happen to you, what would happen to your own anger and need to have the person apologize if you turned and saw that the person who bumped into you was in a wheelchair? Would you focus on the law of apology in your head or try to help the person? Other people standing in the same movie line may have whole sets of private should thoughts about each other. For example, consider a couple standing in front you. "He should pay for my movie if he cares about me" or "She should have known I was too tired to go out tonight," are examples of the types of should statements that fuel anger and unforgiveness in relationships every day. These types of thoughts also pose obstacles to your goal of learning to forgive.

The "All-or-Nothing" Error

When people engage in this type of thinking error, they see the world in absolute, black-and-white terms, for example saying to yourself, "How can I forgive someone who. . . . It's impossible." Do you have any of these "all-or-nothing" thoughts with regard to your own difficulties in forgiving? If so, it's important to practice changing your thoughts to be less all-or-nothing and more accurate. For example, "I can't forgive" could be changed to "It's very difficult for me to forgive" or "I'm really struggling with forgiveness over this." There is an important reason for changing such all-or-nothing internal statements. When you say to yourself that something is impossible, you cease trying (why would any logical person try to do something that's impossible?). The accurate statements of difficulty or struggle, on the other hand, maintain your motivation to continue to try to forgive.

The Overgeneralization Error

When you make the error of overgeneralized thinking, you reach or establish a general conclusion based upon a single incident. This internal statement is often carried as a fact for a very long time, for example, "I'll never forget that he once said to me . . ." This thinking error often occurs in situations where people who have engaged in criminal behavior may be forgiven by their victim or others, much to the outrage of onlookers. For example, a father of a teenager who was killed in a tragic murder visited a prison two years later to talk with a rather infamous serial killer who had, according to many accounts, experienced a transformation and a strong sense of remorse over his past actions. The father wanted to talk with the individual, understand his transformation process, and use the experience to help his own healing process and capacity to forgive. Many people were unable to see the inmate in any other terms than as a brutal murderer. As a result of our own work conducting therapy with convicted sexual offenders, we are often asked, "How can anyone ever forgive such people?" The fact is that many people in the lives of these men, some of whom have engaged in very hurtful or destructive behavior, forgive them each day. In some cases, the individual has changed and earned forgiveness—in other cases, they haven't. It's important to remember that *forgiving does not equal excusing*. The person doing the forgiving, not the offender, is giving the gift of healing to themselves and moving forward with their life.

Now let's return to Bob's story so you can practice identifying the thinking errors that make it more difficult for him to forgive. Then we'll move on to a tool to help you practice identifying your own thinking errors.

Identifying Bob's Unforgiving Thoughts

As we return to Bob's story, we can identify some of the thinking errors described above. These are listed and explained below.

Bob's thought, "I have been successful with my life and Jim hates me for it," is an example of personification. Bob is attributing all of Jim's behavior to himself. In truth, Jim may view himself as a failure and be saying things to himself that are similar to that which he heard from his parents all through the years (for example, "Why can't you be more like Bob?"). Jim probably hates hearing these self-statements in his head and at times (not always), thinks that if Bob weren't so successful, he could argue with his own thoughts more effectively. His anger toward Bob is probably more "lazy" than hateful. It's much easier to blame Bob for his unhappiness than to confront tough decisions about changing his own life. He is also probably still angry at his parents for failing to see his unique strengths, and some of that negative feeling gets transferred onto Bob.

The thought, "How dare he resent my happiness? I was always happy for him," is an example of the should error. Here Bob is essentially saying that Jim should be more like him! Isn't this exactly what Jim has been hearing his whole life? Perhaps Jim is desperately trying to discover who he is and step out from his parents' expectations. In this case, Bob's judgment in many ways resembles their parents' past admonitions for Jim to be "more like Bob." Now, it's true that Jim's choice of hurtful behavior toward Bob has sad and destructive consequences for their relationship, but Bob's difficulty with forgiving Jim's actions are based more on his judgment of how Jim *should* be, rather than recognizing that Jim's choices seem to have worsened the situation.

Bob's thinking, "Brothers should support each other if they love each other. He doesn't love me," is another example of the should thinking error. Notice that there is also an example of the over-generalizization thinking error here, when Bob concludes that Jim doesn't love him. Bob's conclusion that Jim does not love him may be accurate or not. It's difficult to say at this point, because he has not had the opportunity to speak with Jim. However, the fact that Jim attacks him rather than supporting him is much more an indication of Jim's ineffective coping style than his love, or lack of it, for his brother.

Bob thought, "How can I forgive him if he doesn't even think he did anything wrong?" is an example of an all-or-nothing thinking error. Bob's choice to forgive Jim wouldn't mean that Bob is letting his brother off the hook for his nasty behavior (although understanding Jim's actions may soften his view of the behavior). If Bob chooses forgiveness, it's a goal that he must set for himself alone. In the final analysis, it really doesn't matter whether Jim acknowledges a need for forgiveness or not. Bob's struggles are within himself to remove the barriers within himself that make it difficult to forgive and bring him closer to the person that he wants to be. His mind's internal statement that forgiveness is impossible because it's difficult is simply not true. In fact, he knows that practicing challenging tasks is the only way to get good at learning new skills.

Challenging Your Unforgiving Thoughts

Bob's use of the technique below helped him to see that his trouble with forgiveness was based more upon his own tendencies to personalize, overgeneralize, and engage in all-or-nothing and should thinking. When he practiced changing his unforgiving thoughts to more accurate thoughts, he was able to forgive Jim. But this story of brothers doesn't have a perfect ending. In fact, Jim's behavior didn't change very much. Bob, however, approached the family celebration that he'd been so worried about with the following thoughts: "It would be much nicer for both of us if Jim and I could count on each other's support. Unfortunately, Jim's behavior is currently standing in the way of this happening now, and this makes me feel angry and a bit sad. It's my hope that my ability to forgive Jim may change the way he behaves toward me in the future." Bob found that he was able to forgive Jim and reduce the threat of his own anger taking away from his positive experience of the family celebration.

Now that you can learn how to identify some of the thinking errors that are present in unforgiving thoughts, you're ready to move on to practicing this skill with your own thoughts. In order to practice effectively, you'll have to keep a list of the thoughts you have when you are experiencing difficulty forgiving others. For example, the next time you experience a desire to forgive someone but find yourself having difficulty, practice the following steps.

Step 1: List People To Forgive

Take our your journal and write down the name of the person or people whom you'd like to forgive.

Step 2: Acknowledge and Commit

Acknowledge your anger and make a commitment to try and let go of the anger. Write down your feelings and thoughts.

Step 3: Consider the Barriers

Look at the thoughts you've written in your journal that serve as barriers to your ability to forgive. What do you say to yourself as you consider what is preventing you from leaving your anger behind and moving forward? What do you say to yourself when you question why this person possesses so much power? Why does this person's existence and actions cause you to feel so vulnerable? Does your relationship with this person cause you to face some unpleasant aspects of your own inner voices that you would rather avoid?

Step 4: Choose the Hardest

Write down your most distressing thoughts as you consider the previous questions. Now look them over and see if you can find examples of the thinking errors we've just examined. If so, write down any examples that you can find.

Step 5: Select an Alternative

Now, for each thought that contains a thinking error, take the time to consider an alternative thought that is more accurate and balanced. For example, if you find examples of personalization, change the thought to one that considers reasons other than a focus on you that may explain someone's behavior. If you find evidence of shoulds, change the thought to one of "I would prefer . . . , but different people handle things differently." If you find evidence of all-or-nothing thinking, such as "Lying is completely unacceptable," change the thought to one that is more realistic but flexible, such as "Lies between people can have serious, hurtful consequences."

Remember that the changes you make to reduce these common thinking errors may not immediately result in your ability to easily forgive others. However, practicing this technique will help you pave the way for your continued efforts toward forgiveness. It's important to learn to correct these common thinking errors because they currently represent major barriers to your spiritual goal. If you find yourself having significant difficulty separating yourself from such thoughts, practice the mindfulness meditation exercises in chapter 2. Remember that such negative thoughts do not *define you*— just observe them and let them pass.

The 30 Percent Solution

Another tool that can be useful in changing unforgiving thoughts is what we call the 30 Percent Solution. This tool is particularly useful when we see ourselves as totally blameless and are having difficulty forgiving the person who has offended us.

The next time you find yourself angry for more than two days, experiencing difficulty forgiving another person, and ready to make an accusation of blame concerning the problems you experience in your life, remember that in any argument or incident between people, *how you react is contributing at least 30 percent to your current distress.* Even if you have been unfairly accused or treated, you have a choice in how you will react. Regardless of what has happened to you, your choices can probably account for about 30 percent of the reasons why your current emotional state persists. Moreover, your choices regarding how you think and act with regard to this situation will not only impact how you currently feel, but whether or not such situations may occur in the future. Maybe there are ways to think or react differently to reduce the chance of this happening again, or perhaps you have been reacting to what happened in ways that are holding you back from your spiritual journey. Consider the following story about Mary.

Mary's 30 Percent

Although nobody knew it, Mary experienced low self-esteem all her life. Appearing confident and skilled, Mary never shared her fears or vulnerability with anyone, carrying an internal critic inside her that viewed any admission of personal unhappiness as a failure. No one suspected that she was being physically abused by a controlling and troubled partner. Mary reached a point where she went to a women's shelter for help. There, she made a commitment to change her life for the better. She knew that her partner was unlikely to change and decided to end their relationship and start over.

When friends found out about the pain she had endured for the last ten years and applauded her decision to leave, they were surprised to hear Mary say that it was important for her to forgive her ex-partner. They saw it as another act of submission to him and were frightened that if she didn't maintain her anger, she may return to the abuse. What they didn't realize was that Mary was making a much more powerful change. She realized that as disturbed and abusive as her ex-partner was, she had been partially responsible for her past suffering. She viewed herself as trapped in this relationship, fearful that she may not be able to live up to all the expectations others had of her. It had appeared to her that her partner had needed her, and so she hid the abuse from others, choosing to stay with him, and attempting to please him, hoping he would change. This was her 30 percent part in the relationship. *This is not to say that it was her fault.* But realizing that she, too, carried some responsibility for her situation gave her some power. Mary was now able to see that by changing her 30 percent, she could change her life. Her ex-partner no longer had a hold over her and she was able to see his fears and insecurities as part of the factors behind his abuse. Of course, acts of physical abuse in a relationship can never be justified, but by Mary accepting her 30 percent of responsibility for her suffering (and not for her husband's actions—they are two entirely different things!), she was able to focus on the changes she needed to make to leave her abusive marriage and increase her chance of developing healthier relationships in the future.

Applying the Solution to Your Life

Now that you've seen how accepting your share of responsibility can empower you to change for the better, we can invite you to give the 30 Percent Solution a try.

Step 1: List What's Bothering You

Take out your journal. Think about an individual whom you are having difficulty forgiving. Write down the behavior, thoughts, and feelings toward you that you are finding difficult to forgive.

Step 2: Set a Goal

Now use the 30 percent rule to list the behaviors, thoughts, or actions on your part that may have contributed (even just a small percent) to the situation and your bad feelings. List them now and decide which ones you would like to change for the future. For example, if you believe that someone is taking advantage of you, do you ever unintentionally encourage this by not asserting yourself? Perhaps increased assertiveness is a goal for you.

Step 3: Break It Down

Break down your goal for change into small steps and make a realistic plan of action.

Step 4: Reward Yourself

Reinforce yourself for making even small steps toward your goal.

It's important to remember that this technique is not designed to *excuse* the other person's behavior. It is a way to use your difficulty with forgiveness to move you forward toward improving yourself. Studies have shown that even serious self-esteem problems, such as those experienced by women who have been sexually abused, do significantly improve when treated with forgiveness therapy (Freedman and Emright 1996). You will find that as you work to improve your forgiveness skills, you will experience less of a need to hold onto your anger. In the next section, we take this perspective one step further, such that you begin to view your enemies as important to your advancement, rather than something to avoid.

Enemies Are Teachers in Disguise

Do you remember the teachers that you had throughout your life who you would describe as most effective, those to whom you can credit your most significant learning experiences? Perhaps these individuals were school teachers, coaches, art or music instructors, religious instructors, club supervisors, your parents, or other relatives. What made these people effective teachers? What do you remember about the learning experiences they offered that made them so important and memorable?

When most people are asked these questions, they come up with a few key concepts or ideas that express different aspects of the learning experience. First, most people say that effective teachers provide an opportunity for you as the learner to advance and realize your unique potential. Occasionally, they provide an opportunity for you as the learner to accomplish things they knew you could, even when you doubted it. Second, important learning experiences with effective teachers almost always seem to involve something of a struggle, such as learning a difficult subject. Third, when people describe worthwhile learning experiences and important teachers in their lives, they often say that effective teachers give you encouragement and support as part of the experience. Finally, in describing the experience of learning from memorable or effective teachers, many people describe the teacher as one who gives you an opportunity and the guidance to apply what is learned in a practical way. This is a very critical part of the learning experience—when you're encouraged to take advantage of an opportunity to learn and struggle with how to apply this learning to your day-to-day experience.

Would you be surprised to learn that the next time you're confronted with a difficult situation in which you catch yourself blaming or getting very angry at someone who seems to be your enemy, that this could be one of those valuable learning experiences described above? Many spiritual traditions embrace the concept that every person with whom you come in contact during your life can serve as a catalyst for your spiritual learning. Even when someone has committed hurtful and destructive acts resulting in your distress, this concept can still hold true, because your learning is related to your experience and what you take from it. You may want to argue, "But my valued teachers gave me encouragement and support. The current person who is causing me pain, whom I cannot forgive, isn't!" The difference here is that you need to give *yourself* the encouragement and support you need. The individuals who cause you distress still can serve as teachers because they give you the opportunity to learn more about yourself and apply this new knowledge to your own spiritual advancement. It's as if there is a clear and logical reason for why you are presented with this person, in this situation, at this point in time.

Finding Your Teachers

Now you're ready to try discovering surprise teachers of your own. Use the following steps to transform enemies into teachers.

Step 1: Select an Enemy

Take out your journal and write down the name of a person who you currently consider to be your enemy. This could be an individual with whom you have an ongoing battle, such as a family member, neighbor, or a coworker. This person may also be someone that you've met only briefly, but the exchange was warlike and adversarial; for example, the person who hurls angry expletives at you during an incident of road rage or an insensitive and haughty salesperson or secretary.

Step 2: Transform Your View

Assume, for the purpose of this exercise, that the presence of this enemy was actually a type of cosmic gift—that they were being sent by a universal and all-knowing presence to teach you something about yourself, other people, or your connection to them.

Step 3: Consider the Lessons

What can you learn from this experience? Write down your ideas and consider if this life lesson can be applied to other situations in your life. Now think about the other person as being "chosen" to bring you this lesson. Perhaps they were chosen by the universe because their own difficulties and suffering created the very actions that were needed to awaken your insight. If you look at them in this way, even through their actions may still be hurtful, hostile, or greedy, it's difficult for you not to feel some sympathy for them. After all, your encounter with this person has resulted in your spiritual advancement. They have left the encounter with little benefit, other than perhaps to temporarily re-establish their illusion of control.

Step 4: Forgive

Forgive the person's actions, and permit yourself to hope, for their sake, that they are able to change their behavior in the future.

The previous techniques to help you increase your capacity for forgiveness have focused mostly on changing your views or thoughts to be more balanced, accurate, and helpful to you. The next technique has been shown to increase a calm and relaxed body state when you're experiencing the tension of anger in the various parts of your body. As you relax your body, you are better able to move forward in your practice of forgiveness.

Quieting Down an Angry Body: Autogenic Training

Autogenic training is a type of self-hypnosis that was developed over fifty years ago by the German physician, Johannes Schultz. The technique, when practiced, can help to bring about a calming reaction in your mind and body and help you to prepare to let go of negative feelings. This type of relaxed body state can be extremely helpful as you make the changes that are required to carry through with your goals of forgiveness for others, as well as for yourself. At times, even if your head and heart is willing to forgive, your body continues to react with negative energy and anger. Therefore, this tool can be helpful to quiet down your "angry" body.

The standard autogenic training includes focusing on feelings of heaviness, fostering a sense of warmth in your arms and legs, and focusing on your breathing. Your attitude toward the exercises should not be intense or strenuous, but should consist more of the following attitude, "I'm going to tell my body to do this and just let it happen." This tool uses simple phrases to help the body relax and is meant to allow specific physical reactions to occur. For example, the phrase, "My arms are heavy and warm" is meant to increase blood flow to the arms. This tool is really a combination of both meditation and self-hypnosis, but don't be alarmed in hearing the word "hypnosis." This is not the kind of hypnosis that encourages people to act differently (for example, "like a chicken"). Rather, you control what you're doing at all times, and what you are controlling is your own relaxation.

When to Use Autogenic Training

Autogenic training has many applications to improve mental and physical health. It is considered a powerful relaxation strategy and has been used to help calm and manage negative emotions, such as anger and anxiety, and to foster relaxation and stimulate creativity and positive emotions. In addition to the calming effects of autogenic training, which can help alleviate emotional pain and accomplish your goals of forgiveness, it has also been found to be an effective tool for physical symptoms. These include migraine headaches and other chronic pain problems, insomnia, asthma, Raynaud's disease, and coronary heart disease (Stetter and Kupper 2002).

Preparation

You can have a friend or family member with a calm, pleasant voice make a tape-recording of the autogenic script provided in the following paragraphs, or you may want to make the tape yourself. Remember to allow frequent pauses in the script to give yourself time to feel what's happening. You can even add some of your own favorite relaxing instrumental music playing softly in the background. This way, you will be able to have your own autogenic-training tape that you can use over and over again.

Find a comfortable place to practice autogenic training, such as a recliner, couch, bed, or soft floor covering. Remember to loosen clothing, remove glasses or contact lenses (in case you fall asleep), and lower the lights to create a more calming effect in the room environment. Make sure that your legs are not crossed and your head is supported, as your body is likely to experience a sense of heaviness that would be uncomfortable if your legs or arms were in a crossed position. Practice once every day for at least one week. Practicing this tool is important, and like learning any other skill (for example, driving a car, using a computer, playing a piano), the more you practice, the better you get! Trying this tool only once or twice will not produce the kind of results that you want. Therefore, practicing is important. A single session will take about twenty to twenty-five minutes to complete.

Prior to beginning, assess your body for signs of muscle tension. These areas of tension should be targeted as areas to concentrate on while going through a training procedure. In this manner, you can become aware of the specific ways in which this training is helping you to calm your mind and body, allowing you to reach a peaceful place in which to practice forgiveness. Now get comfortable and follow the script provided below.

⁂ Autogenic Training Script

Let yourself go now, getting deeply relaxed all over. Start by taking a deep breath, feeling the air flow in all the way down to your lower stomach and filling your whole abdomen region. Now exhale slowly, and as you do, feel the air slowly releasing from your lower abdomen, and allow yourself to settle down into your chair. Close your eyes and focus on the sensations of breathing. Imagine your breath rolling in and out, like waves easing onto the shore. Think quietly to yourself, "My breath is calm and effortless ... calm and effortless." Repeat this phrase to yourself as you imagine waves of relaxation flowing through your body—through your chest and shoulders, into your arms and back, into your hips and legs. Feel a sense of tranquility moving through your entire body. Continue this for the next few moments (pause now for ten seconds).

This is your time. Don't waste it on thoughts of what you should be doing later or what you have done earlier. Focus only on your own internal voice and what your body is feeling right now. If you find that thoughts intrude, do not dwell on them. You can simply notice them, let them pass, and come back to your own "inside" voice. Let them pass like clouds in the sky. Imagine a white light starting at the crown of

*your head. The light is your essence, your "mind's eye" and will travel
and spread warmth wherever you tell it to.*

*Right now, travel with your mind's eye down to your right shoulder,
into your right arm, and into your right hand. Make mental contact with
your right arm and hand . . . now . . . feel it . . . be aware of it . . . and
notice where your right hand touches the chair. Allow your arm and hand
to become heavy and very warm. Imagine warmth flowing gently through
your hand, wrist, and fingers* (pause now for ten seconds).

*Maintain this mental focus and repeat the following phrase
silently to yourself, "My right hand is heavy . . . my right hand is
heavy and warm . . . my right hand is letting go." Repeat these phrases
to yourself silently for the next several seconds. As you maintain
mental focus with that hand, allow your whole right arm to now
become heavy and warm. Continue to breathe regularly and slowly,
and now say these three phrases silently to yourself, "My right arm is
heavy . . . my right arm is heavy and warm . . . my right arm is letting
go." For the next thirty seconds, repeat them silently to yourself in
your head* (pause now for thirty seconds).

*Notice what your arm feels like now. Is it tingling or heavy?
Does it feel hollow? Is it light and floating? What does it feel like?
Become aware of any tiny sensations and try to describe them to
yourself. Now, using the image of the white light, your mind's eye,
focus on your right arm again. Make mental contact with it. Just allow
it to do the things that you say. Say again to yourself, over and over,
"My right arm is heavy . . . my right arm is heavy and warm . . . my
right arm is letting go." For the next several seconds, keep out all other
thoughts and repeat these three phrases over and over again* (pause
now for thirty seconds).

*What does your right arm feel like? Carefully scan it with your
mind's eye. Try to describe, silently to yourself, exactly what it feels
like. Think to yourself, "If I had to describe what my arm feels like
right now, what would I say? Is there any sensation at all?"*

*As you allow your right arm to stay completely relaxed, travel
with your mind's eye up your right arm, across your shoulders, and
down to your left arm and hand. Make mental contact with it, noticing
where it touches with the chair or material where it's resting. Allow it
to become very heavy and warm. Imagine warmth spreading and
flowing gently through your arm, wrist, hand, and fingers. Maintain
this mental focus and repeat the phrase silently to yourself, "My left
arm is heavy . . . my left arm is heavy and warm . . . my left arm is
letting go." Repeat these phrases silently to yourself for the next few
moments* (pause now for thirty seconds). *As you maintain contact
with that arm and continue breathing regularly and slowly, say those
three phrases silently to yourself, "My left arm is heavy . . . my left*

arm is heavy and warm . . . my left arm is letting go." For the next
thirty seconds, say them over and over silently to yourself (pause
now for thirty seconds). *Note what your arm feels like right now.
Is it tingling? Does it feel heavy and warm? Is it light or floating?
What does it feel like? Become aware of any tiny sensations and try
to describe them to yourself* (pause now for ten seconds).

    *Think to yourself, "If I had to describe exactly what my arm and
hand feels like to someone else, how would I describe it?" Silently use
the words to describe it to yourself for a few seconds* (pause now for
ten seconds).

    *Once again focus your attention on your left arm. Make mental
contact with it. Just allow it to do the things that you say. Say again to
yourself, over and over, "My left arm is heavy . . . my left arm is heavy
and warm . . . my left arm is letting go."* For the next thirty seconds,
keep out all other thoughts and repeat the three phrases over and over
again (pause now for thirty seconds). *What does your right arm feel
like? Carefully scan both arms with your mind's eye. Do you notice any
differences between the right and the left? Is there any spot of tension in
either arm? If so, just allow the light of your mind's eye to spread total
warmth and relaxation throughout both arms and hands. Try to verbalize
to yourself exactly what it feels like. Is there any sensation at all?*

    *Now bring your mental focus to your legs for a few moments.
Imagine your mind's eye spreading a light of warmth and heaviness
flowing from your arms down into your legs. Think to yourself, "My
legs are becoming heavy . . . warmth is flowing through my feet . . .
down into my toes . . . my legs and feet are heavy and warm . . . my
legs and feet are letting go"* (pause now for ten seconds). *Now scan
your body for any points of tension, and if you find some, let them go
limp and allow your muscles to become completely relaxed. Notice how
heavy, warm, and limp your body has become. Think to yourself, "All
of my muscles are letting go . . . I'm getting more and more relaxed."*

    *Take a deep breath. Feel the air as it gently fills your lungs all
the way down your abdomen. As you breathe out, say to yourself,
"I am calm . . . I am at peace . . . I can forgive* (use whatever words
you choose)." *Do this for a few moments, and feel the sense of peace
throughout your being* (pause now for ten seconds).

    *Count to the number 3, and with each number, take a slow, deep
breath and exhale. On the count of 3, slowly open your eyes and adjust
again to your surroundings. Stretch your arms and legs before rising
and returning to your activities* (pause now for ten seconds). *One . . .
slowly get more used to the room around you and know where you are.
Two . . . bring back with you all the feelings of relaxation and calmness
you experienced in this exercise, even though you are becoming more
alert . . . and three.*

Tracking Your Progress

Throughout your use and practice of autogenic training, we suggest that you continually assess your tension level before and after each practice session. You may want to keep notes regarding each session, especially when you're first learning how to use the tool. Don't forget to reward yourself, at first for trying, and then for making progress. Remember—this is a tool that requires much practice before it's really effective. Therefore, don't be discouraged if you don't feel totally calm or relaxed after one or two attempts. The more you practice, the more successful you'll be in helping yourself maintain a calm body and mind to help you forgive.

The next tool provides you with exercises designed to improve your listening skills. We have found that people who can really listen to what other people are saying are less likely to make the thinking errors that we discussed in the beginning of this chapter. We're presenting this strategy last because you're likely to have more success with this skill if you've learned how to keep your body and mind calm while using the technique.

Learning to Really Listen

Although it's not a necessary condition to understand why someone may have acted in a way that hurt or disappointed you, it often helps to understand others' words or actions as a way of gathering information to help test your own thoughts and assumptions and to clear the way to forgiveness. The idea is that if we see where the other person is coming from, although we may not ultimately agree, we tend to see that the other person's actions are usually driven by a personal need on their part, rather than a direct focus on us. This realization helps us to keep in mind that the negative emotions that we are having difficulty letting go of aren't coming from the other person, but are the by-products of our reactions to the other person.

Listening allows us to better understand other people's intent or motivation, reducing our tendency to react automatically. Listening is a skill that is not meant to be used apart from other skills, but, as with any other new skill, it takes practice to improve. Until you learn the skill of listening, you may experience difficulty and confusion in your ability to understand others' intentions. This makes it very challenging to try to determine when the other people in your life are asking for forgiveness or not.

Opening Your Ears

Choose a conversation in which to practice your listening skills. Prepare for the conversation by remembering the following rules. You can even jot down the rules on a card to carry with you in case you forget. When you begin your practice, you will begin timing yourself and follow the listening rules that are provided below for five minutes.

Step 1: Mind Your Body Language

Pay attention to your nonverbal means of communication. A good listener makes eye contact with the other person and leans forward with an expression of interest.

Step 2: Focus

Think of listening as a form of meditation—in other words, take a deep breath, remove all pressure from yourself to respond, and focus on what the other person is saying in the present.

Step 3: Keep a Lid on It

Never interrupt. When most people are engaged in a conversation, they worry about what they will say next instead of trying to hear and understand. Your task for the next five minutes is to simply try your best to understand the other person. They may be stating an opinion with which you disagree or expressing a feeling that you don't share. Right now, the content of what they're saying only matters to you in as much as you try to understand their viewpoint or feelings.

When you find that you have the urge to speak up before the other person has had a chance to finish what they're saying, fight this urge to be preoccupied with your own thoughts. Come back and ask yourself, "What is this person trying to say?" Do not break in with your own insightful, wise, or brilliant comments—do not allow yourself any opinions, but keep all attention on the other person.

Step 4: Merely Reflect

Don't ask any questions, other than reflections back on what they are trying to tell you. For example, you might offer, "Do you mean to say that you . . . ?" or "It sounds like you're feeling . . ." You can try to reflect back on what you've heard by repeating their message, but the only statements you should allow yourself are ones that start with "Do you mean that . . . ?" or "It sounds like your saying that . . ."

Listening Pitfalls to Avoid

❧ Avoid being judgmental. Every time you begin to judge the speaker or give an opinion (even if you agree), silently yell "*Stop!*" to yourself. Your only job during this listening exercise is to reflect and understand, not to have an opinion.

❧ Resist the temptation to turn the conversation into a grilling session of questions for the other person. If you find yourself asking questions eliciting new information rather than clarifying what the person means, then you're not really listening.

❧ Resist all urges to share your wisdom, no matter how insightful or brilliant you think you are.

When you're done with the exercise, take a few moments to consider the difficulties that you experienced while practicing the skill. Some people continually experience a pull to give advice. Other people keep asking questions, because they are having difficulty seeing something from someone else's viewpoint. Others may experience the desire to argue with the person or judge their opinions. The areas where you experience the greatest difficulty are the areas where you need the most to practice.

Carrying Out Forgiveness: Two Plans of Action

Now that you've learned several skills for increasing your capacity to forgive, you will be better outfitted to continue on your journey toward this spiritual goal. What follows are two specific action plans that you can use in order to put these skills into practice.

When Others Ask for Forgiveness

Making forgiveness work to strengthen a relationship is a three-step process. When someone is asking you for forgiveness, you may want to open your heart to allow a connection of love or light between you, but you fear that if you trust them you'll be hurt. The following three-step process will increase the likelihood that another's request for forgiveness and your hard work at forgiving will have positive results for both of you.

> Our anger belongs to us, and it's up to us
> to do something about it.
>
> —Paramananda

Step 1: Listen

Listen to the person asking for forgiveness. True desire to repent and ask forgiveness involves an understanding that we have done something that resulted in another person's pain or injury. A person who is truly sorry or experiences regret is aware that their behavior, whether intentional or not, resulted in another person's suffering. Your listening skills will become very useful here because you have practiced your ability to see through another's eyes and truly hear what they're trying to say.

Step 2: Determine Their Goals

People who seek forgiveness should be clear about their goals. When they are truly remorseful over what they've done, they communicate a sense of certainty that they don't intend to choose the same behavior in the future. For example, an adolescent who apologizes for staying out several hours past curfew and states "I'm sorry" is less likely to be asking forgiveness than another who is able to communicate an understanding of the consequences of his behavior on his family. Although the person's actions resulted in unpleasant consequences for others, they would not have engaged in the behavior if there wasn't some benefit. Ask people requesting forgiveness to indicate why they are certain that they will not engage in the same behavior in the future. If they are asking for forgiveness, they will be certain that they do not want to choose the same path.

Step 3: Appraise Their Commitment

Asking for forgiveness requires a commitment. The person who seeks forgiveness is essentially expressing a commitment to react to the same or a similar opportunity for negative action with a different choice. Indeed, most people are given numerous opportunities to face situations that represent the core choice of a behavior they want to change. For example, consider the person who has reduced their own fears of being criticized or laughed at by taunting or criticizing someone else. Although they may not be confronted with the opportunity to hurt the same person in the same way, it is likely that they will face similar situations where they can choose to reduce their fears in alternative ways, rather than at someone else's expense. Ask the person who is requesting forgiveness to tell you how they will manage their behavior when faced with similar choices and situations in the future. In order to make the changes that follow their request for forgiveness, they will need to have a plan for future behavioral choices in place.

Remember that the actual act of forgiving is not a gift you bestow on the other person, but a gift you give to yourself. However, by following the steps above and listening carefully to the person asking for forgiveness, you will have some estimate of how likely the person is to engage in the same behavior again. This will help you determine whether or not they are committed to working on their relationship with you.

When You Ask for Forgiveness

The same action plan for forgiveness is important to implement when you're the person who is seeking forgiveness. Specifically, as you follow steps one through three, you will answer the questions yourself regarding your awareness, your clear intention to not repeat the same behavior, and your commitment to doing things differently in the future. Is there a past thought, behavior, or action for which you want to be forgiven? Perhaps there are thoughts, feelings, or behaviors of which only you are aware and are having difficulty forgiving yourself. Write a statement in your journal concerning your awareness of how such incidents may cause the suffering of another. Now write down your clear intentions to change the thought, feeling, or behavior. Finally, write a realistic plan of action of what you will do the next time you're confronted with a similar situation.

When Others Don't Seek Forgiveness

When others do not ask to be forgiven, is it still important to have a plan for forgiveness? Absolutely. There is an old saying that, "The man who is intent on revenge must dig two graves." Learning to forgive does not mean that you will continue to allow others to hurt you or that you will put yourself in the position to be hurt. Forgiveness does not mean that you are saying it was okay for the other person to take the actions that they did. The critical message inherent in the spiritual goal of forgiveness is that when you forgive, you remove your focus from the incident and its consequences. You focus instead on moving yourself forward. Forgiveness does not mean justification or forgetting—it means that you are letting go of your anger, opening your heart to heal, and creating peace in the present moment. These are positive steps toward awakening your self-esteem.

A man that studies revenge keeps his own wounds green, which would otherwise heal and do well.

—Francis Bacon

Step 1: Get Out of the Situation

If you remain in a situation in which you are continuing to experience emotional or physical pain or hurt, remove yourself from the situation. For example, if an angry neighbor is shouting obscenities at you because of an ongoing resentment, walk into your house, away from the attack, and shut the door.

Step 2: Get Calm

Practice the autogenic training or other relaxation/meditation exercise to put your body in a calm state.

Step 3: Review Your Options

Consider your options to prevent future attacks or hurt.

Step 4: Consider the Source

Understand the attack as coming from that person's disability, desire for power, control, greed, or any other obstacles to their own spiritual advancement.

Step 5: Let Go

Make a conscious choice to let go of your anger and forgive the other person.

Step 6: Shift Your Energy

Place your energy into healing and caring for yourself and for others.

Finding the strength to forgive is one of the most challenging of life's spiritual goals. The rewards of forgiveness to your self-esteem and sense of well-being, however, are certainly worth the effort.

CHAPTER 6

Increasing Patience

Through training our minds with constant effort,
we can change our mental perceptions or mental attitudes.
This can make a real difference in our lives.

—Dalai Lama

Patience as a Spiritual Goal

Patience is an important spiritual goal because it provides a way to help us abide the provocations, major misfortunes, and minor annoyances that are part of life. When we increase our patience, we increase our tolerance of adversity without complaint and reduce the urge toward restlessness and anxiety when confronted with a delay in getting what we want. Examples of the powers of patience are frequent in the life stories of well-known inspirational figures. The Buddha revealed a response of patience and compassion toward a brother who tried to kill him, whereas Jesus showed an understanding patience toward his disciple Peter when Peter, out of fear of what would happen to him, denied the existence of their relationship.

Patience and Self-Esteem

When you are patient, you have learned that you can make it through the turmoil and chaos of your life situations. This can have enormous impact on your goal of self-esteem and sense of well-being. If you're confident that you will not only get through and survive a provocation or misfortune, but that it's likely that you will actually retain an insight, lesson, or worthwhile experience from it, imagine how your self-confidence in your ability to handle whatever comes at you can be increased!

People who are spiritually enlightened and maintain a strong sense of self-esteem are often seen by others as happy and at peace. What others don't see are the moments, days, weeks, and years of continuous learning, struggle, and practice that is involved in each person's journey. Indeed, many people often assume that spiritual struggles for the "enlightened" are a matter of the past and that coping with life has become easy for them. Although continual practice of techniques that move our spiritual goals forward will often improve our insights and awaken self-esteem, each journey requires a strong and continued sense of patience with ourselves and others.

The Seduction of Instant Gratification

As our lives become full of technology, we increase the demands we place on ourselves and others to deliver immediate gratification. Consider the difference between your expectations ten years ago as compared to the present. We now expect to be able to talk with someone immediately on their cellular telephone. We expect an answer to our e-mail from anywhere in the world within twenty-four hours (or less!). When we travel away from our jobs for a few days to spend time with our family and or friends or to be by ourselves, we are never far from our faxes, telephones, digital cameras, or e-mail. We can meet business associates, romantic partners, and sales clerks through the virtual reality of our computers. All of these changes have reinforced our greedy tendencies to want things now and expect to get things fast.

The urge to get everything faster and easier has extended to a demand to control our fear or our pain. We want and demand immediate relief and quick fixes to our self-esteem problems such as power, drugs, alcohol, money, or sexual attractiveness. Drug companies, plastic surgeons, and spas have been doing record-breaking business catering to these desires. Unfortunately, such quick fixes are often ineffective in truly impacting our self-esteem. Without the patience and hard work of inner change, no immediate gratification will ever be enough. Yet, such solutions can be very attractive when you experience a tendency to lose patience with the amount of time and work involved in more long-term, but truly effective, solutions.

> **Patience is the companion of wisdom.**
>
> —St. Augustine

This is why we provide this chapter. It's designed to increase your insight regarding the importance of patience and provide you with techniques to increase your motivation to persevere as you continue on your journey.

One way that psychologists can help people to increase their patience is by working with the body first. Tools that focus on changing the sensations in your body to create a calming and relaxed state can set the stage for your mind to accept that good things take time. If you are able to calm your body and relieve tension, you experience less urgency to do something quickly to get relief. When you experience impatience with yourself or others, you can feel the sensation of tension and urgency in your body. The following tool will teach you how to relieve the tension through practice.

Muscle Relaxation for a Patient Body

Systematic Relaxation Training, also known as Progressive Muscle Relaxation Training, was first described by Dr. Edmund Jacobsen, a Chicago physician, as a technique to reduce physiological tension in the muscles (Jacobsen 1938). Since Dr. Jacobsen first developed and promoted this technique, many physicians and psychologists have demonstrated that this is a very important tool to enhance both physical and mental health. The theory behind how it works is based on the idea that when we experience stressful thoughts or feelings, our bodies respond with muscle tension. This tension in the muscles then gets interpreted by our brains as a signal of more stress and anxiety. This begins a vicious cycle in which we experience a sense of urgency to get rid of the feeling.

Progressive muscle relaxation releases muscle tension and gives a feeling of warmth and well-being to the body. This relaxation is interpreted by our brains as "everything is okay." It's impossible to have our body physically relaxed and experience anxiety at the same time. Therefore, deep muscle relaxation, when successfully learned, can be a very strong natural medicine to increase your patience and to help you calmly proceed on your journey.

Use of this tool takes practice at first, but becomes easier after you learn to do it. If you want to learn this technique, it's important that you practice it once every day for at least two weeks. Practicing this tool is important because, like any other skill, the more you practice, the better you get! Trying this tool only once or twice will *not* produce the kind of results you want. Therefore, practicing is critical. A single session will take about twenty to twenty-five minutes to complete.

Muscle relaxation training has been evaluated in many research studies and found to be an important form of stress management. Excellent results have been found for the treatment of a wide range of stress-related disorders and medical problems (Carlson and Hoyle 1994). In other words, it's a very powerful tool!

In a calm voice, tape-record the relaxation script provided in the next few pages. This way, you'll be able to have your own muscle relaxation tape that you can use over and over again.

In your journal, write down the dates that you practiced progressive muscle relaxation and after scanning your body for the current level of tension that you're experiencing, write down the current level of tension in your body on a rating scale of 0 (no tension) to 10 (the most tension your body can experience). At the end of your practice, write down the level of tension that is currently in your body. Any residual tension will be an important place to focus on during your next relaxation training session. First, here are a few reminders or helpful hints to make your relaxation training more successful.

* Find a comfortable spot to practice this tool, such as a recliner, couch, bed, or soft floor covering.

* Loosen clothing, remove glasses or contact lenses, and lower lights.

* Make sure your legs are not crossed and your head is supported.

* Rate your current level of muscle tension.

* Take note of your tension level before and after practice session.

❧ *Muscle Relaxation Script*

*Allow yourself to take a big, deep, breath and relax. Say to yourself,
"I am going to let go of tension . . . I will relax and smooth out my
muscles . . . I will feel all of the tightness and the tension dissolve away."
Now we will begin the progressive muscle relaxation procedure.
Your first muscle group will be your hands, forearms, and biceps.
Clench your right fist . . . tighter and tighter . . . study the tension and
discomfort as you do so. Keep it clenched and notice the tension in
your fist, hand, and forearm. Hold this tension in your right fist for
a few seconds* (pause, letting the tape record silence for three
seconds). *Now relax. . . . Feel the looseness in your right hand. Notice
the contrast with the tension. Repeat the procedure with your right fist
again, always noticing as you relax that this is the opposite of tension
. . . relax and feel the difference.*

*Now clench your left fist . . . tighter and tighter, studying the
tension and discomfort as you do so. Keep it clenched and notice the
tension in your fist, hand, and forearm. Hold this tension in your left
fist for a few seconds* (pause now for three seconds). *Now relax . . .
feel the looseness in your left hand . . . Notice the contrast with the
tension* (pause now for five seconds).

*Now repeat the entire procedure with your left fist, clenching
tightly and holding* (pause for three seconds). *Relax. Now try both
fists at once. Clench both fists . . . tighter and tighter, studying the
tension and discomfort as you do so. Keep them clenched and notice the
tension. Hold this tension in both fists now for a few seconds* (pause
here for three seconds). *Now relax . . . feel the looseness in your
hands . . . allow warmth and relaxation to spread all through your
hands.*

*Now bend your elbows and tense your biceps. Tense them as hard
as you can and observe the feeling of tension and tightness* (pause for
three seconds). *Now relax . . . let your arms straighten out. Let
relaxation develop and feel the difference between the tension and strain
in your arms. Now repeat this procedure. Bend your elbows and tense
your biceps. Tense them as hard as you can and observe the feeling of
discomfort* (pause now for three seconds). *Now relax . . . let your
arms straighten out. Let relaxation develop and feel the difference
between the tension and strain in your arms when they were tensed
and how they feel when relaxed.*

*Your next muscle group will be your head, face, and scalp.
Turning your attention to your head, wrinkle your forehead as tight
as you can* (pause here for three seconds). *Now relax and smooth it
out. Imagine that your entire scalp is becoming smooth and relaxed . . .
at peace . . . at rest. Now frown and notice the tightness and strain*

spreading throughout your forehead (pause now for three seconds). *Now let go . . . allow your brow to become smooth and soft again. Close your eyes now and squint them tightly. Squeeze them closed. Notice the tension and any discomfort* (pause for three seconds). *Now relax your eyes and allow them to remain gently closed* (three-second pause). *Now clench your jaw, biting down hard. It should feel like trying to hold something in your teeth* (pause for three seconds). *Now relax your jaw. When your jaw is relaxed, your lips may be slightly parted and you will feel your tongue loosely in your mouth. Now press your tongue against the roof of your mouth. Feel the ache this action creates in the back of your mouth* (three-second pause). *Now relax. . . . Feel your tongue soft and loose in your mouth. Now press your lips into an "O," as if you were blowing bubbles (pause now for three seconds). Now relax your lips. Notice that your forehead, scalp, eyes, jaw, tongue and lips are all relaxed* (five-second pause).

The next muscle group will be your head, neck, and shoulders. Press your head back as far as you can and observe the tension in your neck. Bring it back to center, then roll it from right to left, noticing the changing location of the stress. Straighten your head forward, pressing your chin to your chest. Feel the tension in your throat and the back of your neck (pause here for three seconds). *Now relax . . . allow your head to return to a comfortable position. Let the relaxation spread over your shoulders and deepen* (three-second pause). *Now shrug your shoulders. Keep the tightness and tension as you hunch your head down between your shoulders. Feel how uncomfortable this position is (pause for three seconds). Now relax your shoulders. Drop them back and feel relaxation spreading throughout your neck, throat, and shoulders, pure relaxation, deeper, deeper* (five-second pause).

The next muscle group will be your chest and abdomen. First, give your entire body a chance to relax. Feel the comfort and the heaviness. Now breathe in and fill your lungs completely. Hold your breath and notice the tension (pause for three seconds). *Now exhale. . . . Let your chest and abdomen become loose while the air is coming out. Continue relaxing and let your breathing become calm and natural* (three-second pause). *Repeat the deep breath once more and notice the tension leave your body as you exhale* (five-second pause).

Now tighten your stomach as if your were trying to "suck it in," making it hard and flat. Hold it there (three-second pause). *Notice the tension. Now relax. Arch your back (without straining). Notice the tension in your lower back and hold this position for a few seconds* (pause now for three seconds). *Focus on the tension in your lower back. Now relax, gently straightening your back down and relaxing all over* (five-second pause).

Now you'll work on your legs and buttocks. Focus your attention on this muscle group. Tighten your buttocks and thighs. Flex your thighs by pressing your heels against the floor as hard as you can (pause for three seconds). *Relax and feel the difference* (three-second pause). *Now point your toes like a ballet dancer, making your feet and calves tense. Study the tension and hold it* (pause now for three seconds). *Now relax . . . notice the difference between the relaxed feeling in your legs and the discomfort that you experienced a moment ago. Bend your toes toward your face, creating tension in your shins. Pause and hold it* (three-second pause). *Now relax again* (five-second pause).

Feel the heaviness and warmth throughout your lower body as the relaxation spreads all over you. Relax your feet, ankle, calves, shins, knees, thighs and buttocks. Now let the relaxation spread to your stomach, lower back, and chest (pause for three seconds). *Let go more and more* (three-second pause). *Experience the relaxation deepening in your shoulders, arms, and hands. Deeper . . . and deeper. Notice the feeling of looseness and relaxation in your neck, jaw, and all your facial muscles* (three-second pause). *Say to yourself, "My muscles are relaxed, warm, and smooth . . . I am letting go of all my tension . . . I am deeply relaxed . . . my muscles are relaxed, warm, and smooth . . . I am letting go of all my tension . . . I am deeply relaxed." Enjoy these feelings of relaxation for the next few moments* (two-minute pause during which reader can occasionally say, "More and more relaxed, deeper and deeper into relaxation").

Now bring your focus back to the present time and place while I count from one to five. With each increasing number, try to become more alert to your surroundings. Open your eyes, but keep the feelings of relaxation in your body (slowly count from one to five).

Tracking Your Progress

As we mentioned earlier, it's important to record your tension level before *and* after each relaxation session. You can then track how well this relaxation tool is working for you. If you don't experience changes in the beginning, consider how patient you've been at working on the tool. Skills such as Progressive Muscle Relaxation take a little bit of time and practice to be helpful. Therefore, you can begin to increase your patience as a function of giving yourself time to learn the tool.

Reward Yourself

Increased patience and decreased levels of stress, depression, pain, and anxiety can be a powerful reward for learning this relaxation tool. However, remember that you should reward yourself for

taking the time and effort to learn. When you begin relaxation training, set a goal for practice (for example, once a day for the first few
days). When you have accomplished this goal, give yourself something that you enjoy as a reward.

A point to remember in using this tool—some people may
become distracted and not able to complete an entire progressive
relaxation procedure for the first few sessions. Don't let this stop you.
Just follow the procedure for as long as you can and stop whenever
you want to. Over time, you'll find yourself becoming less distracted
and able to stay with the procedure for longer periods of time.

Learning to relax your body can be a powerful antidote to the
urge for instant relief from day-to-day hassles and major life problems. In other words, this tool can help you increase your patience in
response to any type of stress. Although Progressive Muscle Relaxation will work well if you ask someone that you trust who has a
pleasant, calm voice to read the instructions to you, making a tape of
your own voice may provide you with increased confidence, knowing that you have the power to help yourself.

This relaxation tool helped you to focus your energy on helping
your body to be more patient. However, even with an increased confidence to calm your body, you may be still concerned about the times
when you experience strong, negative emotional reactions that make it
difficult to be patient with yourself or others. Managing negative feelings is one of the most common complaints we hear from people who
are trying to learn to be more patient with problems they are
facing—"How can I stop and try to understand what I want to change
when I'm overwhelmed with all these feelings?" It can be hard to see
how increasing your patience with your own feelings can help you to
be wise. The next tool is designed to give you added wisdom by
helping you to be a "better listener" to what your feelings are trying to
tell you.

When you practice using the next tool, you will discover not
only that you can become more patient with your feelings, responding to them in less automatic and potentially maladaptive ways, but
you may actually begin to look to them as an important source of
your wisdom.

Understand the Wisdom of Your Feelings

Psychologists have designed this important tool to help people like
you better manage strong emotions. By using this tool, you can
increase your patience and use your feelings to your own advantage.

"Using Feelings as Cues" is a step-by-step approach that will help you to:

❊ Increase your patient understanding that feelings (even powerful or upsetting ones) are normal,

❊ Recognize your feelings when they happen,

❊ Use your emotions to work for you, rather than against you, and

❊ Know what is really important to you.

People experience distressing feelings every day, but they are often tricky to predict. Sometimes our feelings are a reaction to just one situation or thought, and they simply pass. Other times, we're bothered by upsetting feelings for a long period of time. Problems like depression, anxiety, anger, and bereavement all involve distressing feelings.

Sometimes the feelings are even more troublesome or made worse if we have different emotions at the same time. For example, we may get angry and start hitting things or yelling at people, even though we are actually feeling afraid or sad. If this has ever happened to you, you are likely to find this tool especially useful. In addition, sometimes we may feel dissatisfied or guilty about the way we express our feelings to other people. For example, some people may be very quiet and unresponsive with their spouse or partner, not because they want to be hurtful, but because they're not sure how to handle their strong emotions. Again, if this describes you, this tool can be very helpful. Finally, some people try to block out or avoid upsetting emotions by using drugs or alcohol. Unfortunately, this is only a quick-fix solution that wears off quickly. There are other options! Offering you these options is the purpose of this tool.

Learning to be Wise

The following step-by-step instructions for "Using Feelings as Cues" will teach you to direct the power of feelings to your advantage. By practicing these steps, you will be more aware of your negative feelings and able to use them as cues to help you understand more about how you want to manage your life situations. You will have greater patience for your feelings because you will find them useful.

First, take out your journal. Record the information requested in each step. Begin each entry by noting the date and time.

Step 1: Notice Feelings When They Happen

Throughout the day, any time when you begin to feel distressed, stop and notice what you're feeling and how intense it is. Remember the phrase "Stop and be aware" from chapter 3? This technique can be useful here as well. Try to put the feeling into words, writing them down in your journal. Notice where you experience this feeling the most. Do you have physical sensations, a pounding heart, a lump in your throat, or a flushed face. Do you say things to yourself like, "I can't take this," "I don't need this," "I hate to feel this way," "I'll show him what it feels like," or "I give up"? As you begin to get familiar with how you experience your own emotions, consider both the physical sensations and things you say to yourself as cues.

Step 2: Record Your Distress Level

Simply record your emotional distress level in order to help you be more aware of how you're feeling at any given time. This will help you to know where you stand and allow you to monitor your progress. Use a scale from 1 to 10, where 1 represents total peace of mind and tranquility, and 10 represents the most distressed you could possibly become. Then go immediately to Step 3.

Step 3: Stop and Be Aware!

Here is your chance to increase your awareness. Imagine a stop sign or a flashing red traffic light as a way to help you stop. This step means stopping what you were doing, almost like pressing the "pause" button on your video player or movie camera. During this small break, you should:

❦ Make sure that you recorded your level of distress, and

❦ Label and describe the emotion you are feeling in your journal.

Now think about the important information that you are receiving from your emotions. This step is geared to help you increase wisdom—enabling you to better understand what your emotions are trying to "tell" you. In general, your brain is capable of two different kinds of processing, emotional responding and logical thinking. When you react to situations only with your feelings, it's difficult to listen to the logical or rational part of your mind. In this case, you're likely to act impulsively with even more and/or stronger feelings. For example, if you're feeling hurt because someone ignored you, you may react automatically with anger or fear before you even have a chance to understand why you're feeling hurt.

On the other hand, if you think only with logic, you may disregard the important information that your emotions are providing you. For instance, suppose that you're feeling very sad because you are lonely. Your rational thinking may lead you to discount or discredit your feelings, which may lead you to be unaware of the importance of seeking more support or friendship from others.

What happens when we bring emotions and rational thinking together? Patience! We believe that it takes *both* types of processes to be wise and patient—in other words, to be able to use your emotions to let you know what's really going on. This can be hard work, because it means allowing yourself the time to figure out what important information your feelings are providing you. With this new wisdom, however, you'll be able to answer the question of what your emotions are telling you. More importantly, having this information allows you to decide what to do next.

What Do Your Emotions Know?

Look at table 7, "The Feelings Detective: What Your Emotions May Reveal." We provide this table as an important reminder for you to actually ask yourself this question. Remember why you have emotions in the first place—to give you information! Your body is hard-wired to react with certain feelings for very good reasons. Consider the following examples. You experience fear when there is a danger to which you must react in order to keep safe. You experience anger when you want something but are being blocked from what you want. You experience sadness when you lose something or someone and must accept a change of some kind. You experience a combination of anger and sadness when another person or situation is responsible for your loss.

Table 7. The Feeling Detective: What Your Emotions May Reveal

Feeling Type: Fear

Information to look for: Any sense of threat or danger

Examples of what the information may reveal:

- ❦ Fear of physical injury

- ❦ Fear of being laughed at

❊   Fear of being inferior (examples include: intelligence, talent, physical skill, outward appearance)

Feeling Type: Anger

Information to look for: Being blocked from what you want—the block can be due to circumstances or specific people

Examples of what the information may reveal:

❊   Wanting success or to be the best

❊   Wanting a relationship

❊   Wanting an accomplishment

❊   Wanting to be loved or admired

Feeling Type: Sadness

Information to look for: Losing something or perception that you are losing something

Examples of what the information may reveal:

❊   Losing a person (such as a friend, lover, or partner) in one of the following ways—a move, illness, death, disagreement, the person choosing other people to be with, or losing a role or status

Feeling Type: Embarrassment

Information to look for: Revealing your vulnerabilities

Examples of what the information may reveal:

❊   Others can see your imperfections, mistakes, and problems

Feeling Type: Guilt

Information to look for: You regret something

Examples of what the information may reveal:

❊   You have hurt others through your actions

❊   You have not done anything wrong, but you or someone else is telling you so

The Feelings Detective table also contains the type of information you should be looking for when you're trying to identify what your feelings are "saying" to you. In this table, we have also provided a few common examples of what the information may reveal.

Some of the information emotions provide may point to an actual situation that you'll need to do something about. It may also involve something that you are telling yourself, and your emotional reactions are based on these thoughts. Other information may suggest that you must face a new situation or change. If your emotions point to a situation where negative thinking may be responsible for the negative feeling (for example, "I didn't get the raise because I'm stupid!"), you can use the tools in the book that are designed to help you change negative thinking patterns (see chapter 4). If what you're saying to yourself is based upon true facts (for example, the death of a close family member), consider using the tools that provide you with ways to increase your joy or your social support to help you get through difficult times (see chapters 2 and 4).

Listening to Your Feelings Increases Patience

In order to achieve emotional balance and focus on future decisions and activities that are important to you, you must learn to actually "listen" to your emotions and then apply your logical thinking skills to decide what changes they're asking for. In other words, to use your *wisdom*. Remember that we define wisdom as the ability to use your emotions and rational thinking together. Trying to avoid or block emotions out only makes the situation worse. Here are a few questions to ask yourself as you patiently listen to your feelings.

※ Allow these emotions to occur and pass. Do not try to rush them away—just notice them, let them quietly happen, and pass by. Here would be a good time to practice the mindfulness meditation exercises described in chapter 2.

※ Do you need to calm your emotions? If so, consider using one of the other tools in this book designed to trigger a calm and tranquil physical state. Tools available are breathing meditation, visualization, or a relaxation exercise, such as the one you just learned.

※ Do you need to make a spiritual or psychological change in your life? If so, go to the chapter in this book pertaining to the changes for that particular spiritual goal—one or more of the tools may help.

❦ Are you afraid? It's important to remember that feelings are not only normal, but they are actually precious pieces of information about what is happening to you. In this way, emotions help us to determine what we need to do next.

As we mentioned earlier, it's important to record your distress level when you experience strong emotions. You can then track how these levels may be changing when you use this new tool. It's quite possible that you will experience what other people have reported—that you learn to appreciate and use your feelings in a way that helps you to be less distressed and overwhelmed. In other words, you still will experience strong emotions, but are becoming more patient with your feelings.

Using your feelings as cues and experiencing a better understanding of your negative emotions can be a powerful reward in and of itself. However, remember that you should reward yourself for taking the time to increase your patience. When you begin using your feelings as cues, set a goal for practice (for example, plan on using your new wisdom several times per week). When you have accomplished this goal, give yourself something that you enjoy as a reward.

Now that you have increased your wisdom concerning how to read your own emotions, it's important to learn ways to use these feelings to help you grow and awaken your self-esteem. Next, we move to a tool that combines the goal of seeking help from a Higher Power with a psychological technique using the memory of powerful emotional experiences to help you heal and continue on your path towards self-esteem.

Seeking Help for Patience

Seeking guidance from a Higher Power, regardless of your personal spiritual beliefs, usually consists of silent or outspoken verbal communication with a supreme source of power, knowledge, or inspiration. Such words most often take the form of humble requests, statements of thanksgiving and gratitude, or honor and praise. As such, this connection to our Higher Power provides us with the opportunity to share spiritual faith with others or give expression to what we are feeling, needing, or hoping for. The actual activity can take the form of prayer, meditation, or even communing with nature. Each spiritual philosophy and set of teachings may pose a slightly different interpretation of how or why prayer, meditation, and communication with a Higher Power offers psychological, emotional, and health benefits for many people.

To everything, there is a season,
A time for every purpose is under heaven.

—Ecclesiastes 3:1,4

Respecting and valuing these different perspectives, we provide here a more psychological explanation of the benefits of this communication. This in no way either disputes or validates any other spiritual views of why or how prayer works. The tool that we provide in this section is based upon psychological research and can be used in addition to any specific prayers or meditations that are part of your own spiritual beliefs. Through the use of the following tool, we recommend that you seek help through a letter to your Higher Power as a way for you to abide and withstand the painful and traumatic moments of your life.

Many people equate prayer with requests for things that are questionable or unreachable. This type of prayer often focuses upon requests to change the outcome of life situations, such as reducing our distress or improving our good fortune. For example, people use prayer for everyday events such as passing academic tests, winning sporting events, or safe driving, to much larger events, such as surviving a surgery or cancer treatment, preserving a marriage, or curing a drug addiction. In such cases, the person praying is asking their Higher Power to grant their request in a merciful and benevolent gesture. Other common uses of prayer involve some form of negotiation, for example, "Lord, if you take away this pain, I will learn to be more patient," or "God, if you help me get through this, I will be more giving and less greedy." In such cases, people making these types of prayers have made the assumption that their current trials reflect a punishment—that is, the negotiation is a statement that they have heard this "message" and are willing to change. In these instances, communication is used to let the Higher Power know what you're willing to do to be granted your desire.

Many people believe that it doesn't make much sense to assume that we need to inform our Higher Power of our needs. In fact, many individuals say that any true Higher Power would already probably know what was needed and that this power wouldn't need to be convinced that we are sincere in our prayers. In fact, most patients we've spoken to who report great benefits from prayer seem to focus more on the comfort or insight derived from prayer and less on the outcome of specific requests for material products. Rather than embrace an unrealistic expectation that prayer can protect you from experiencing the inevitable pain and tragedy that is a part of life, many see prayer as the way to patiently move forward with their lives, *despite* the presence of such pain and tragedy.

We have spoken to many family members of medical patients who have died even though many people prayed for them to get well. Both of us have personally shared similar experiences in our own lives as well. Most people who continue to maintain a strong spiritual focus do not believe that their prayers have been ignored when tragedy occurs. Rather, the focus of their prayer shifts to one for help with acceptance and guidance in navigating the grief and loss. This is consistent with the popular Serenity Prayer that asks for "the power to change what one can, acceptance of what cannot be changed, and the wisdom to know the difference." This simple prayer, repeated daily in thousands of meeting groups for individuals coping with substance abuse problems, can help us to achieve a patient sense of balance in our life situation—a balance of both its mortal limitations and infinite joy.

Trying to increase your own personal understanding of and patience with this balance may lead you to communicate with your Higher Power, however you define it (him or her), in a way that advances you on your spiritual journey. We hope that the tool we provide next will help you to accept and understand the painful experiences in your life while remaining open to the possibility of miracles in your LIFE. This perspective of prayer as a reminder of the pain we must accept, as well as a hope for the miraculous, makes sense from both a psychological, and spiritual point of view.

How Prayer Can Help

We know from the work of many behavioral scientists that expressing painful emotions in written and verbal form can have a profound impact on both psychological symptoms and physical health. Expressive psychological therapies include techniques that are designed to increase a person's awareness and expression of emotions. Written emotional disclosure, for example, refers to writing about thoughts and feelings with regard to personally stressful and traumatic events. This type of expressive therapy has consistently demonstrated positive effects on psychological well-being, mood, physical functioning, and general well-being. Scientific studies conducted by researchers who specialize in psychoneuro-immunology (the science of how the mind and body interact in health and illness), have shown that when we experience strong and distressing emotional reactions, putting them into words can serve to organize our thinking, make some sense of what we want to change in ourselves or in our life situations, and foster our ability to remain open and optimistic. The very act of communicating our deepest and most private feelings in a safe and nonjudgmental environment to a listener who we perceive as wise, understanding, and caring can therefore have very healing and therapeutic effects for a wide range of emotional and often physical pain.

Researchers differ in their explanation of why emotional disclosure through writing or talking about a distressing event seems to be important to one's mental and physical health. Some believe, based upon what is called *conditioning theory,* that the more you expose yourself to a stressful topic or situation, the more you become accustomed to your thoughts and feelings about it. This process is known as *habituation,* where one's body becomes so used to the distress that it no longer reacts to what once was a distressing event in a distressed manner. Others propose that when people repress or inhibit emotional reactions or stressful memories (for example, purposefully not thinking about one's negative thoughts and feelings), they exert significant mental and physical energy. This energy drain can then result in significant psychological, emotional, and medical consequences. Releasing these emotions and memories frees this energy and relieves the strain.

There are many studies that measure physical stress responses when people either share or hold back their thoughts and feelings about a stressful event. These studies support the idea that confronting stressful events through writing or verbally speaking about them can enhance our understanding and acceptance of the distressing event and decrease our need to hold back and inhibit our thoughts about it. As a result, we experience improvement in both physical and emotional health (Pennebaker 1995; Schnicke and Resick 1993; Stone et al. 2000).

The next tool is adapted from similar techinques pioneered by psychologist James Pennebaker (1995) in his studies that have shown the positive health benefits of disclosing one's emotions when confronting stressful circumstances or having difficulty coping with negative events from one's past. We suggest that you practice this technique once a week for three weeks, then take a break from the practice for about two weeks, and assess both your mood and the usefulness of the tool. Of course, we're not suggesting that you limit your conversations with your Higher Power to this technique alone, only that you make a point to practice it several times in addition to any other prayer or meditation you find helpful.

Step 1: Find a Private Place to Write Your Letter

Find a quiet place where you will be free of distractions (children, other people, telephone, etc.). You will need approximately twenty minutes to complete this technique, and you shouldn't be interrupted. When you're seated and ready to begin, set a timer or alarm clock for twenty minutes.

Step 2: Write a Letter to Your Higher Power

Write a letter to your Higher Power in which you take the opportunity to write about one of the most upsetting or traumatic experiences of your life. You can write in either your own handwriting or a use a typewriter or computer.

Step 3: Express Your Deepest Emotional Concern

Choose an event that had a deep, traumatic effect on you. It can be a recent event or one from a long time ago—only you know what is truly upsetting to you. Common examples include writing about the death of a loved one, the break up of a romantic relationship, or a personal failure. The important thing is that you write your deepest thoughts and feelings about the event. You should have no concerns about grammar, spelling, punctuation, sequence, or length. What's most important is that you really delve into your deepest thoughts and feelings about the event. Ideally, whatever you write about should deal with an event or experience that you haven't talked about with others in detail or may be hesitant to disclose. *Remember, no one will see this but your Higher Power and you.* Stop writing after twenty minutes and put the letter in a private place.

Step 4: Write Two Additional Letters

Repeat the procedure two additional times. Your writing exercise should be about the same experience all three times and separated by several days to a week.

Step 5: Read the Letters Aloud

After the final writing exercise, privately read aloud what you have written. Then describe to your Higher Power (either silently to yourself or out loud) where you continue to need help and guidance in placing this event in context and learning from it for the future. Write down what you think you learned from this event. How will understanding this event help you to be more patient with yourself in the future?

Step 6: Evaluate Your Progress

Assess the usefulness of the technique in helping you experience greater patience toward the painful and traumatic moments in your life. If you found it helpful, follow the same steps anytime you believe that seeking this type of help from your Higher Power enhances your spiritual advancement.

Now that you have tools to help you increase your patience with your body and emotions, the final tool will help you to increase your patience through your thoughts.

Practicing Waiting: A Meditation for Patience

In today's world, we are frequently required to wait. Think about all the situations in which you have spent time waiting in the past month—grocery lines, bank lines, airport lines, waiting in a line to buy tickets, waiting in line to park or wash your car, waiting in traffic lines, waiting on lines in amusement parks, restaurants, buffet lines, tourist offices, unemployment, the Department of Motor Vehicles, the post office, the doctor's office, and so on. You realize we can go on and on—just like some of the lines that you've had to endure.

We think these situations provide you with a great opportunity to practice a waiting meditation. Imagine the different view you may take the next time you're faced with a long line if you looked at it as an opportunity to spend some time doing something for yourself!

Step 1: Change Your View

The next time you encounter a line, make a decision to engage in a waiting mediation. Make a self-statement, recognizing your good fortune and expressing silent gratitude for the opportunity to quiet your mind, practice patience, and take the time to look inward.

Step 2: Clear Your Mind

Using the instructions for the Mindfulness Breathing Meditation from chapter 2, clear your mind and allow yourself to become aware of all the thoughts, feelings, and urges that come into your head. You may observe statements that your mind has learned to say about having to hurry. You may feel frustration or irritation with someone else's behavior in the line. If so, just observe them without judging, and let it pass.

Let any thoughts or feelings occur and pass, bringing yourself back to the moment by saying to yourself, "I am waiting. I am aware."

Step 3: Refocus

As you sense your waiting period end, refocus your attention to the tasks that must be done. You will notice that there are times that you actually experience a resistance to have to pull away from this quiet moment to yourself.

You have probably noticed that it is easier to be patient when waiting if you're having a good time (that's a no-brainer!). Last year during a holiday rush for fresh pastries, we arrived at a Philadelphia pastry shop that is famous for its fresh, creamy cannolis, a favorite Italian pastry. The line was already about fifty yards long and growing by the minute. The staff, who had, through years of experience, grown accustomed to such long holiday lines, moved at their own pace with no sense of urgency. People in the line had cell phones, coffee, newspapers, portable radios, and CD players. They talked with each other and held each other's place in line if someone needed to use the restroom or attend to a parking meter. There was a sense of community and holiday fun that pervaded the scene. When the line was shown on the television news, there were people who had been delighted to be part of this newsworthy happening!

The waiting meditation works on a similar principal. The difference is that in this case, the fun and excitement of the waiting experience is the chance to experience the joy, the energy, and the gratitude that is inside you. Try it! You may also wish to engage in a Wabi-Sabi-type experience while waiting on line (see chapter 3).

CHAPTER 7

Creating Hope

For lo, the winter is past, the rain is over and gone,
the flowers appear on earth.

—Bible (Song of Solomon)

The Spiritual Goal of Hope

Have you noticed that spiritual goals encourage us to strive for our best rather than focus on the despairs of life? For this reason, hope is an essential spiritual goal. In our lives, we continually face change and challenge. There may be times when you find yourself saying, "And just when I thought things were going well, this had to happen. I give up." Sometimes, no matter how hard we work at accepting our negative emotions or vulnerabilities or to find a solution to a problem, something happens to make the job even more difficult. In such situations, we need hope to inspire us to focus on what's possible in spite of these obstacles. For example, as we have witnessed with many patients confronting death from cancer, hope can be present until someone draws their last breath. Even during the worst of times, spiritual coping during stressful events can help mitigate the effects of even serious illness. In such cases, hope for a physical cure may no longer be the goal. Rather, hope for emotional healing, hope for repaired relationships, hope for one's legacy, or hope for peace remain critical goals to self-esteem and to well-being.

Hope Is Crucial to Self-Esteem and Well-Being

In Emily Dickinson's famous poem entitled Hope, she personifies hope as a little bird "that perches in the soul" (1976). The image represents the small and seemingly fragile part of us all that relentlessly endures harsh times and whose song can be heard through gale-force winds and storms. This vision of hope provides an insight as to the importance of this emotion to self-esteem. Hope represents the expectation that all will eventually turn out well. It's important to point out that creating hope does not mean expecting the impossible. It means that even when your expectations and desires aren't met, you have the ability to focus on some positive aspect of your experience and "know" that it will have some positive outcome. You know this to be true because you believe in your ability to make it happen. This focus keeps your attention on the strength of who you are and the benefits of your spiritual journey. As explained by psychologists Andrew Tix and Patricia Frazier (1998), who have studied how religious faith helps people to cope, spiritually-oriented people pay more attention to positive psychological outcomes and life satisfaction and less on trying to reduce symptoms of pain and distress when faced with tough life situations.

Psychologists who study hope, such as C. R. Snyder (2000), have defined it as a positive emotion or feeling that consists of two important parts: first, the belief in our ability to find workable and realistic paths to our goals, and second, the motivation to continue on our path to such goals. The first part includes our ability to think optimistically. Thinking optimistically helps you to manage tough obstacles, disappointments, and adversity by expecting more positive outcomes in your life. Hope takes optimism even one step further. When people are hopeful they actually use adverse events to give them information they need to stay with their goals and consider alternative pathways to reach them. Finally, hope includes motivation to continue on a chosen path. Both optimism and hope are important skills to have when you're faced with life's problems. Note that we characterize these as "skills" rather than simply feelings, as they can be learned, increased, and enhanced.

Tools for Creating Hope

The tools provided for this location on your journey are aimed at increasing both elements of hope. They include learning to use two new tools, Turning Obstacles into Opportunities with Optimism and Creating Beliefs of Hope, through the discovery of creative ways to pursue your goals. Your motivation to continue on your path toward goals will be helped with the use of a tool we refer to as Unpacking Your "But" Baggage, as well as another visualization technique. We now turn to our first tool, which uses optimistic thinking to help you turn obstacles into opportunities.

Optimistic Thinking

When following the biographies of successful people, a common theme that emerges is perseverance in the face of obstacles. This perseverance is often fueled by a sense of optimism. Psychologist Martin Seligman (1998) has described an optimistic thinking style as one in which people make *external, variable,* and *specific* attributions for the negative events in life, rather than *internal, global,* and *stable* causal explanations. For example, while working on his spiritual goal of reducing his anger and need to compete with others, Andrew, a police officer, heard that his partner, Steve, had gotten the promotion to lieutenant that they'd both applied for. Angry at being passed over and guilty over his reaction to his friend's promotion, Andrew experienced the following *pessimistic* thoughts.

    ❦ "I guess I'm not as smart as Steve."

    ❦ "I was stupid to think they would promote me—I'm not political enough."

    ❦ "I'll be walking this beat forever."

Compare these thoughts with the following *optimistic* thinking style.

    ❦ "I'm disappointed, but Steven's a good man, and his skills matched this placement."

    ❦ "This particular post seems pretty political, it may not be the best match for me."

❊ "I've learned a few things that will help me get a good shot at the next promotion."

It's not surprising that, in the first case, Andrew's pessimistic thoughts might result in hopeless despair because his explanation for his disappointment attributed the cause to global and internal failures on his part (lack of skill and stupidity), global and stable (unchanging) personal external obstacles (politics and favoritism), and belief that things will always be this way, with no ability to change them.

On the other hand, if Andrew's thoughts were more optimistic, it's likely that he would explain the disappointment as due to a specific situation and external circumstances (regardless of Andrew's own strengths and ability to do the job, this one specific appointment involved a strong political component for which it was predictable that Steven was a good match), and a variable situation (not all appointments are subject to the exact same set of circumstances). It's easy to see how pessimistic verses optimistic thinking could lead to feelings of hopelessness and depression for Andrew over not receiving the promotion. However, by viewing the situation in terms of one particular circumstance and looking for ways to increase his positive outcomes in the future, Andrew could be engaging in optimistic thinking and be able to turn his obstacles into opportunities.

In the face of adversity, disappointments, obstacles, and failures, an optimistic person persists. We refer to this characteristic way of thinking as "realistic optimism" because it doesn't mean that you tell yourself things that aren't true in order to feel better. Rather, it means that you focus your thinking on *how you can help them come true*.

The Battle for Good and Bad Inside Your Head

There is a battle for "good" and "bad" inside each of our heads. Psychologist Roy Baumeister and his colleagues (2001) suggest that the bad force is often stronger than the good one in our internal struggle. For example, negative emotional experiences such as getting in a car accident or experiencing a loss tend to have a longer-lasting impact than positive emotional experiences, like winning the lottery. This phenomenon may be partially due to the fact that as human beings, we have evolved to avoid any kind of pain and suffering as part of our survival. Thus, we tend to keep ourselves focused or tuned in to the possibility of any negative or painful experiences that may occur. The irony here is that we end up being especially sensitive and frightened of such experiences, and their destructive strength is maintained. In contrast, nurturing positive internal experiences like optimism and positive emotions takes extra effort, because our natural tendency is not to be so tuned in to them.

Now consider the mood shift that will occur if you view obstacles, disappointments, and suffering as an opportunity to grow and strengthen your spirituality. This is actually an ancient idea in that it's part of the way that stressful obstacles are viewed in the Chinese language. Looking at the written symbols that make up the word that the Chinese use to express "stress," the first character would translate as "danger." The second character, if viewed separately, would translate as "opportunity." These Chinese characters reflect how hardships and suffering can be viewed as both danger *and* opportunity.

Practicing Optimism

In the following technique, we provide a way to restructure your natural internal reactions to disappointment, discouragement, and setbacks on your spiritual journey, replacing them with images and thoughts of optimism. Take out your journal and follow the steps below.

Step 1: Choose Your Challenge

Think about a current challenge or negative event that you're facing and write it down. This may be a disappointment, such as a failure or a desire for something that you can't have, a loss, a painful experience, a medical challenge, a frustration, or a rejection.

Step 2: Review What You Wrote

Read over what you wrote about this challenge and examine it for any evidence of internal, global, or stable characteristics. As you read, look for any places where you may be attributing the obstacles that you're facing as due to something that: 1. is due to a basic fault of you or another person; 2. is a very global and pervasive statement about you or another person; and 3. is stable, in other words, impossible to change. For example, one patient we know, Tracy, was trying to work on increasing her optimistic thinking about her mother after the recent death of her father. She wrote the following words in her journal, "My mother will never get over this—and I know me—I'll start to feel bad about having any fun in my life. It's never going to change. I miss my father, too, but my mother needs to have someone to take of, and how she is alone. I've never been able to make her happy." You can see from Tracey's journal entry that she appears hopeless because her thinking is attributing the problem to internal problems that are very pervasive and unable to change.

Step 3: Switch to Optimism

Now change the statements to reflect optimistic thinking. The secret weapon of optimism is to change your thoughts to ones that remain realistic but are more flexible in seeing the specific, external, and variable characteristics of the situation. For example, when Tracey changed her thoughts, here is what she wrote in her diary:

> My mother is having a difficult time coping with my father's death. In this situation, she provided care for such a long time that she's become quite accustomed to that role. When I see her feeling sad and confused, I have a habit of thinking that I must make things better. I even start feeling badly if I can't make everything right. This is one of those situations in which I feel a pull to fix things. My father's death will be difficult for all of us. I know that there is much to figure out, but I believe that it will get better with time and that my mother and I will work these problems out.

If you're having trouble with this part of the tool, remember that you are not supposed to have *only* positive responses to the situation. Just be looking for what specifics about this situation may be different than others, how there may be several reasons for why it exists, other than the fact that it's *all* your fault, and that it's possible that the current causes are changeable. Remembering these guides helped Tracy to get "unstuck," and she was able to ultimately come up with the above entry.

Step 4: Practice, Practice, Practice

Make plans to practice your new way of thinking. Now that you know how to make your thoughts more optimistic, practicing this new realistic optimism will help you to turn the obstacles in your life into opportunities. Tracy reported that this experience helped her learn that she could show love and concern for her mother without blaming herself and contributing to the hopeless expectation that things would never improve.

The miraculous aspect of this technique is that no matter how or what the life challenge or obstacle, you can *always* remain optimistic about the future. In the next tool, Creating Beliefs of Hope, you will discover that any goal may have many paths and learn ways to keep your motivation alive in order to meet your goals.

> **Hope is patience with the lamp lit.**
> **—Tertullian**

Creating Beliefs of Hope

As a first method for creating hope, we want you to take out your journal once again and write at the top of a page, "The Many Paths to My Goals." Next, take a few moments to think about a current spiritual or other goal that is important to you. This could be a goal with regard to something you wish to accomplish, such as getting a new job, or a spiritual goal, such as learning to forgive someone who has hurt you. We recommend that you use this method whenever you experience a loss of hope in reaching your goals. In order to practice the method, think about one of your current goals. When you have a goal in mind, proceed to the first step.

Step 1: State Your Goal

Write down your goal in your journal. Try to be as specific as possible.

Step 2: Find Your Progress

Think about any way, large or small, during the day that you moved toward your goal. At first you may think that you haven't done anything to proceed toward the goal, but we know you have. For example, even the fact that you wrote down the goal in your journal represented time that you spent thinking about your goals and reminding yourself of your commitment to reach the goal!

As an example, let's look at Dave's journal about showing more compassion toward others. In other words, he wanted to make his thoughts, feelings, and actions more consistent with trying to understand and relieve the suffering of others. For Dave, this meant learning to express compassion for all people, even those who he may traditionally envy, such as his wealthy boss, or dislike, such as his brother-in-law. He was experiencing some discouragement and disappointment with himself as he struggled toward this goal. He originally hoped to work this year for a national charity organization where he'd be able to experience a major advance toward his goal. But he'd just found out that his wife had lost her job and he'd have to work extra hours at his accounting job in order to make ends meet. He decided to use Creating Beliefs of Hope in order to help boost his expectation that he would still be able to advance toward his goal in the future.

Here is a summary of the daily journal list Dave wrote down after just one week. He listed anything he could think of that helped him toward his goal of greater compassion, even though he was unable to work for the charitable organization.

❧ Saw television movie about the work of Mother Teresa (reminded me of the incredible result of the compassion of one person).

❧ Talked with a friend about why compassion is so important (how it helps both the giver and receiver).

❧ Made a commitment to develop a list of ways to show more compassion at work (even in the accounting business, there are many ways that I can understand and help alleviate the suffering of others).

❧ Made a point to notice the extent of suffering on the commute home from work (to remind myself that there are so many people who can benefit from compassion).

❧ Focused my attention on one of these observations, a couple who was evidently arguing, and decided to try to show greater compassion to my own wife.

❧ Listened carefully to the problems of my teenage son (made attempt to understand why he's currently feeling frustrated with his schoolwork).

❧ After talking with my son, thought about how I might teach him to be more compassionate (as I listened to his complaints, I realized that he was very focused on his own achievements and tended to be insensitive to peers).

❧ Committed myself to trying to teach son compassion (realized that I may be of some help in shaping my son's way of relating to others).

❧ Bought a book by the Dalai Lama on compassion (to increase my knowledge and understanding).

❧ Read a few pages of the book on compassion (fell asleep after reading four pages—but at least got four pages read).

❦   Thought about times in my life that compassion from others would have helped (to increase my motivation to help others).

❦   Searched the Web for additional opportunities to help other charitable foundations (to find more alternative paths to pursue in the future).

As you can see, Dave is discovering that his original goal of infusing his life with more compassion has many alternative paths than the original one he intended. Although his original plan was good, when his life threw him a curve, he began to create hope that he would still accomplish his goal by considering other paths. By continually brainstorming about the many different paths and routes to your own goals, you increase your hope that you'll eventually reach that goal. In addition, you increase your daily motivation to persevere.

Another way to help you to increase your motivation is to take the time to actually develop a list of the benefits you'll gain if you are able to successfully continue on your journey, as well as a list of potential outcomes if you were to give up on your goals.

The Motivational Ledger

In this brief but useful tool, you will develop a motivational list for you to use that will remind you of the positive outcomes of reaching your goals, as well as the negative consequences of giving up on your goals.

Step 1: Determine Consequences

In your journal, choose a page and write "My Motivational Ledger" at the top. On the next line, write down one of your goals. Then go ahead and draw a line down the center of the page, forming two columns. At the top of the first column, write down "What will happen if I give up hope and don't pursue this goal?" At the top of the second column, write down "What will happen if I maintain hope and continue to try to reach my goal?"

Step 2: Make a Reminder

Don't try to complete this list all at once. Each day upon getting up or before going to sleep, take a look at the list and see if you can add anything to either column. After working on the list for several days, take the page out of your journal, or copy it, and post it where it will help remind you of your goals. This could be on the refrigerator or bathroom mirror, on a small card on your car dashboard, or in your purse or wallet.

We have a few additional tools that may be helpful to you in maintaining a hopeful viewpoint. For those of you who found yourself more hopeful after using the tools you've learned so far, these additional strategies will help you to *stay* hopeful. For those of you who are still experiencing some difficulty turning hopelessness to hope, these strategies may give you the extra edge you need to boost hope. The first involves a sincere attempt to try to remove the word "but" and "can't" from your vocabulary. We call this Unpacking Your "But" Baggage.

Unpacking Your "But" Baggage

Consider the following example. If you overheard someone saying, "I really need to make a stop at the grocery store on my way home from work, but with the bad weather and traffic, it's going to be difficult at that time of night," do you think that the person is likely to go to the store, no matter how badly they need the groceries? Most people don't think the person saying this will make it to the store.

Now imagine that you heard the same person say, "I really want to make a stop at the grocery store on my way home from work because I'm out of so many things. With this bad weather and traffic, it's going to be difficult." When we ask people this question at workshops and seminars, most agree that in the second case, you would predict that the person will have some difficulties, but is likely to go through with the shopping trip. The only real difference here is that we took the word "but" out of the statement.

There are similar examples to understand the real meaning behind the word "can't." For example, the word "can't" is often used to say that a person is incapable of an action. However, many times when we say "can't," we actually mean that we're *choosing* not to do something because we find it difficult. "I can't talk to my wife," more likely means "I won't talk to my wife because it's difficult to communicate and I'm likely to be uncomfortable."

When we recommend removing the words "but" and "can't," we don't actually mean for you to absolutely remove them from your vocabulary. However, we think that it's important for you to become more aware of the words you use when you say things to yourself that stand in the way of hope. People often use the word "but" or "can't" as an excuse for why they'll give up hope. For example, "I'm committed to improving my health, but quitting smoking is just too hard," versus "I'm committed to improving my health, and quitting smoking is one of the hardest parts!"

Step 1: Prepare Your Card

For this exercise, you'll write in your journal at the end of each day, but you will also need a small piece of paper or card to carry with you in your purse, pocket, or wallet to help you keep track of how many times you use the word "but" or "can't." Finding or making this card is your first step.

Step 2: Not "Buts" and "Can'ts"

For several days, just observe and record how many times you use the words "but" and "can't" when referring to any goal-related behavior (even silently to yourself). Mark the number down on the card that you carry with you. When you get home, write a little more detail about the situations and statements in which you used these words.

Step 3: Replace Them

Try repeating statements similar to the ones in which you used "but" or "can't," but replace those words. Common replacement words for "but" include "and," "in addition," "also," and "at the same time." Common replacement words for "can't" include "won't," "choose not to," or "don't have the patience to deal with." If you find that what you mean when you say "can't" is that you don't have the patience to deal with something, you may want to review chapter 7 for ways to increase your patience.

The fewer excuses you give yourself to give up hope for even small goals, the more successful you'll be in creating hope with the larger goals in your life.

> He who does not hope to win has already lost.
>
> —Jose Joaquin Olmedo

A final tool for creating hope is to create a visualization of your hope for the future. In chapter 2, you learned to use all of your senses to create a future visualization that helped you to identify your spiritual goals. Now, we suggest that one way to maintain your motivation and hope for reaching any of your goals is to practice a different type of visualization, this time to enhance your sense of hope. You may want to refresh your memory regarding the ways to learn visualization and practice using all your senses in order to increase the effectiveness of your visualization.

Visualizing Your Hope for the Future

You can really boast your ability to stay with any goal and maintain hope if you use your visualization skills to keep you focused on the future outcome. For example, visualization has been used this way when individuals are studying hard to reach educational goals, working hard at staying fit or sticking to their diet, keeping hope up for finding a job, or believing that challenging relationship issues can be worked out.

Think about the last time you were in a movie theater and watched a trailer for a new film. The sights and sounds in front of you may have captured your imagination and led you to make plans to return to enjoy this new movie. When writing this book, there were many times that we created a visual image of the various goals and chapters, imagining the words we would use or the real-life examples that would let people know that they aren't alone on their spiritual journey. This visualization sustained us when we were pulled to work on other projects, had more research to do, had patients to see, or simply wanted to walk away from the computer. The following instructions provide you with a brief set of instructions to apply the visualization skills you learned in chapter 2 to help you create an additional experience of hope for *your* future.

First, write a descriptive picture of your goals for the future in your journal. Next, identify the points along the way to your goals where you may begin to lose hope. Now, remind yourself of why it will be important to maintain hope for your goals. Close your eyes and describe to yourself a visual picture of what you will experience when you reach your goals. Remember to use all of your senses to fully experience what it will be like. What will it be like in terms of smell, touch, sounds, and texture? For example, if your goal is to have more quality time with your family, your visualization would include how you and your family would look, what your voices would sound like as you talk or laugh, how you would feel to each other as you hug or embrace, and how the food you're preparing or eating would smell. By putting yourself there, with all your senses, you actually experience the positive outcome as a kind of preview or "coming attraction."

As you visualize your goals, your mind creates a vision of hope that can help you through some of the major obstacles or disappointments along the way.

We end this chapter with another inspirational quote about hope. "Love is not envious or arrogant or rude. It does not insist on its own way; it is not irritable or resentful; it does not rejoice in wrongdoing, but rejoices in the truth. It bears all things, believes all things, hopes all things, endures all things. Love never ends" (St. Paul in I Corinthians).

CHAPTER 8

Awakening Your Self-Esteem

Be lamps unto yourselves.

—Buddha

The Spiritual Goal

In this chapter, we provide the final tools to help you fully awaken your self-esteem. These build upon the previous chapters and tools, but focus specifically on enhancing your feelings of self-worth and awakening your self-esteem. Self-esteem is not commonly identified as a specific spiritual goal, but we view it as critical to your overall spiritual journey because it will help you to stay committed to a life-long (or LIFE-long) trek, long after you finish reading this book. With your self-esteem awakened and now possessing an improved sense of well-being, you are likely to continue on this spiritual journey with a sense of joy, adventure, and challenge. In many ways, this is a new beginning to the rest of your life.

Self-Esteem versus Self-Importance

Many spiritual belief systems distinguish between a sense of true self-esteem and self-importance. The latter is considered to be a shortcut to self-esteem and often serves as a temporary way to cover up our deep fears about our worth. This kind of quick-fix can become a very strong habit, similar to the need for immediate gratification that we talked about in chapter 7. When we take a short-cut to self-esteem by building up our self-importance, the experience rarely lasts very long and requires a continual search for more things to enhance our sense of self-importance, simply to cover up our fears. One tell-tale way to identify self-importance as opposed to self-esteem is that with self-importance we usually experience a need to compare ourselves to others, and we get angry when others fail to recognize how "special" we are. Although it's common for people to take us for granted or fail to recognize our worth, people with a strong sense of self-esteem don't have to prove it to others.

Psychologist Nathan Brandon (1992), who has written many books on the topic of self-esteem, has suggested that there are "no shortcuts to high self-esteem." In order to achieve an increased sense of self-worth, we must first awaken our consciousness, take responsibility for ourselves and our feelings, and face the fact that self-esteem is made up of what we think and feel about ourselves. Rather than viewing self-esteem as the reputation we have among other people, it is more accurately described as *the reputation we have with ourselves*.

A Definition of Self-Esteem

True self-esteem consists of two parts: *self-acceptance*, which is an appreciation of your value and worth as a human being; and *self-confidence*, or the knowledge that you are competent to use your gifts wisely. Awakening self-esteem is hard work because it requires both of these components. With regard to self-acceptance, doubts about our own worth or fears of criticism and ridicule are often well learned over the course of our lives and difficult to change. Many of the tools provided throughout this book represent opportunities to foster an acceptance of your worth and to increase your spiritual awareness in order to enhance this self-acceptance.

With regard to self-confidence, other tools that we've given you for your journey were strategies adapted from well-researched psychological therapy techniques, such as relaxation training, changing negative thinking, managing feelings, improving listening skills, identifying problems, and increasing the joy in your life. These tools can be helpful to you as you continue to face the challenges of your life situations. We encourage you to use them frequently and continue to use your journal as an effective way to maintain practice with the tools you've learned.

How We'll Awaken Self-Esteem

The tools in this last chapter will help you to increase both self-acceptance and self-confidence in order to help awaken your self-esteem and improve your well-being. The first two tools work best when used together and in the sequence they are presented. First, you'll read about a tool called Attitude Training that helps shift your focus away from distressful feelings to an attitude centered on loving self-acceptance. After practicing the first tool, you'll learn the next strategy, called Problem Solving. We have personally invested much of our careers researching Problem Solving over the last two decades and have conducted many scientific investigations that demonstrate its effectiveness in helping a wide range of people who have experienced a wide range of problems.

The first tool will help you focus your awareness on your internal emotional experiences and to use a special set of breathing instructions centered on your heart in order to shift your attitude. This shift will help calm your body and create a feeling of loving reassurance that will help you make the most effective use of any of the tools provided in this book, including problem solving. Both tools are especially helpful when you are experiencing self-doubts about your ability to handle life problems and their overwhelming emotions they often inspire.

How Does Emotional Reaction Work?

When you experience a stressful problem, you encounter something that sets into motion an amazing sequence of mind-body reactions. We use the term "mind-body reaction" to indicate that, in an instant, a complex set of internal physiological and biological events occur. Whenever you experience a threat to your well-being, your mind identifies the threat and your body prepares to do whatever it takes to either conquer it or escape it. As you can see, your body's reaction to stress can be considered a gift, as it provides you with the ability to survive in emergencies or life-threatening situations. This survival reaction, often called the "fight or flight" response, involves many different parts of your brain that are needed for attention, recognition, arousal, understanding and analysis of the situation, emotional experience, and planning of consequent action. In addition, the reaction involves many bodily responses, such as changes in your muscles, increases in hormones and brain chemicals, and increases in breathing and heart rate.

All of these mind-body reactions occur simultaneously, but here's the catch—they don't *only* happen when you're truly in a life-threatening situation. They happen throughout the day, whenever you experience what you perceive to be a threat. This includes threats to your security or safety (for example, when you worry about war, crime, or driving accidents), threats to your self-esteem (when you experience failure, embarrassment, or rejection), and threats to your need to be with others (when you have arguments or experience loneliness). We want to underscore the point that although your stress reaction is part of your hard-wiring, it is likely to be triggered *less often* if you don't see all of these events as a threat to your survival. You can see how important it is to awaken your self-esteem so that you experience more confidence in yourself and fewer threats to your worth as a person.

Now that you have some idea of what takes place when you're experiencing a mind-body stress reaction, let's move on to the first tool, which is designed to short-circuit this reaction when it occurs and provide you with more time to think about what to do to effectively face the challenge in front of you.

Let Your Heart Be Your Guide

Rollin McCraty and his colleagues at the HeartMath® Institute in Boulder Creek, California, have developed a number of scientifically-tested tools, including Attitudinal Breathing, Heart Lock-In, and Freeze-Frame. These strategies can help people to regulate their emotional and physical response to stressful situations. The physical part of the response pertains to changes in heart-rate variability that is associated with a reduced risk of cardiac events. The research from HeartMath® supports their hypothesis that shifting focus to a positive mental state during an emotionally stressful experience is an important key to being able to effectively offset the mind-body reaction to the daily stressors we face.

We believe that the tools from this group may provide a very effective way to put your reactive mind and emotions in check—to help stop, shift attention, and think more effectively about the problems you confront in your day-to-day life. Doc Childre, HeartMath's® founder, suggests that you use Attitude Breathing to help release tension in any part of your body (Childre 1994). Below are step-by-step directions that we have adapted from his instructions for *Attitude Breathing*. We encourage you to practice this tool, and when your practice is rewarded with a shift of attention to loving self-acceptance, you're ready to move onto the next tool, that of problem solving.

Attitude Breathing

The purpose of this tool is to help calm yourself when experiencing anxiety, anger, or sadness in response to a stressful problem. The breathing technique is designed to bring your body back into balance and reduce excess negative emotion by anchoring your energy in your heart and solar plexus region. This will help you stay "centered" in order to use the problem-solving tool more effectively. The instructions are below.

Step 1: Notice the Negative

Become aware of the negative thoughts and feelings that you're experiencing. Now shift your attention to your heart and solar plexus (stomach) area. The solar plexus involves a network of nerves at the upper part of the abdomen behind the stomach and in front of the aorta (a main heart artery).

Step 2: Get Positive

Develop an inner attitude that includes positive self-statements, such as "I will focus on an attitude of joy and self-acceptance," "This will calm my body and mind," or "I can make peace with this."

Step 3: Breathe

Next, gently and sincerely picture yourself actually breathing in this new attitude "through your heart." Then breathe it out through the solar plexus and stomach to anchor it. Do this for several minutes until you can feel the new attitude set in. This may seem strange at first, but keep trying.

> **Ask questions from the heart and you will be answered from the heart.**
>
> —Native-American proverb

Step 4: Commit

Make a commitment to maintain this attitude as you move on to using the problem-solving tool. When you are ready, take out your journal in preparation to use this new strategy.

Problem Solving

Because modern-day life is full of big and small problems, we know that you'll have no difficulty finding problems on a daily basis to help you practice with this tool. In order to become familiar with each step, we recommend that you start practicing the steps we provide below at first with problems that are especially complicated or distressing.

In order to start your practice, take out your journal and write down a problem on which you want to work. Next, rate your current level of distress associated with this problem on a scale of 1 to 10 (1 being the lowest possible amount of distress and 10 the highest). While practicing this tool, note your level of distress on a weekly basis until the problem no longer causes you distress (ratings of 1, 2, or 3).

Now you're ready to begin using problem-solving skills in a systematic way. This tool can be used to make two kinds of important changes to help you solve your problems: 1. changing your own emotional barriers to problems; and 2. changing the actual problematic nature of stressful situations. When tackling a problem that is associated with strong feelings, you also need tools to help you manage strong feelings.

When people face difficult problems, they usually experience a whole range of feelings like fear, shock, sadness, anger, and loss. It's important to learn how to use these feelings to help you solve problems, rather than continuing simply to experience them as overwhelming. Your use of the Attitudinal Breathing tool you just learned, as well as similar tools that help you manage your feelings (for example, Using Your Feelings as Cues) should help you feel more calm and better accept and understand the negative emotions associated with the problem you're facing. However, here are some additional guidelines that will help you use your emotions in a positive way when solving problems. One way of stating this is to *make your emotions work for you, rather than becoming a slave to your emotions.*

Overcoming Emotional Barriers to Problem Solving

❊ Hold off making decisions while experiencing very intense emotions.

❊ Think of your emotions as signals such as a red stoplight, letting you know that you're experiencing a problem that needs to be solved. It's very important that you don't immediately try to get rid of these negative feelings but take some time to use a tool like mindfulness breathing to become aware of your emotional experience rather than acting impulsively on it.

❊ In additional to Attitude Breathing, this book contains many useful tools for quieting down your physical reactions so that you can think more clearly. Relaxation, Autogenic Training, Mindfulness Breathing Meditation, and Visualization are all ways to create a safe and peaceful mind. Problem solving requires that you be yourself, become aware of your inner essence, and understand yourself better.

❊ Writing down your feelings or explaining them to someone who is objective can help to get a more realistic perspective on these problems.

❊ Reviewing the tool Using Your Feelings as Cues from chapter 7 can also be very helpful.

Now you're ready to learn the important skills of problem solving. We present these skills in six steps. First, we'd like to give a you few important guidelines to remember as you practice these steps.

Focus on One Problem at a Time

Some people are eager to solve all their problems at once, but that's often not possible. In fact, self-confident problem solvers will tell you that it's important to take on one problem at a time. As you practice problem solving, try not to skip from problem to problem, but focus on one just problem.

Reward Yourself for the Effort, Rather than the Outcome

When you have the ability to examine your strong emotions (such as fear, sadness, and anger) to help you understand the problems you're facing, it's important that you recognize how important it was to take this step, and reward yourself for the effort. By using your feelings in this way and then following the problem-solving steps below, you are likely to reduce the severity and number of problems in your life. Even reading this section of the book today required you to make a change. Reward yourself as soon as you finish reading this chapter, rather than expecting too much change all at once.

Try to Keep Your Focus on the Now

Many people dwell on past difficulties and hurts when they are feeling distressed, sad, anxious, or angry. These past difficulties can't be changed, and they can be like fuel for negative feelings, turning your emotions into a bonfire. Instead, focus on what you'd like to change in the future. Only use past problems, insults, and hurts to help you decide what goals or life changes are important now.

The Six Steps to Problem Solving

Although many problems appear complex and overwhelming, the average person can learn to solve their problems more effectively by using this tool for making changes in the nature of the problem itself. We have found that solving many of life's problems usually requires a combination of changing our own emotional reactions to the problem, as well as changing the problem situation itself. The six steps described next provide the overall method you can use to change the nature of the problem so that it's no longer a problem.

You can't stop the birds of sorrow from flying overhead. But you can stop them from building nests in your hair.

—Chinese proverb

Step 1: Check Your Problem-Solving Attitude

It's important to maintain a positive attitude about solving your problem. The way you think about your problem can have a strong effect on what you actually do to solve it. Remember the advice we gave you about preparing for problem solving by holding onto a realistic optimism. In other words, when you decide not to avoid a problem and are willing to try some creative thinking about it, then you can actually improve the situation. If you're having trouble developing or maintaining a positive problem-solving attitude or continue to believe that you can't learn to effectively solve problems, review Changing Negative Thinking, Using Feelings as Cues, Optimism, and Creating Hope to help you overcome such negative thinking. If you find that you're losing a positive attitude, feel free to use your attiudinal breathing throughout the remaining steps.

Step 2: Understand the Problem

There is actually scientific truth to the old saying that "A problem well-defined is half-solved." This is because problems that are vague or not clearly defined become more troublesome and frustrating than necessary. Some of the previous techniques we provided can be of particular help in learning to define problems effectively. For example, in chapter 3 we provided instruction regarding how to increase your awareness of problems. The following are important elements of accurately defining a problem that you're faced with.

Get the facts. Try to get as much information about the problem as possible in order for you to better understand what's going on. Think of yourself as an investigative reporter or police detective investigating your problem.

Describe the facts in clear language. For example, after receiving criticism at work Jane's reaction was "My boss hates me! I feel so stupid. I'm never going to succeed at work." A more accurate and factual description might be: "It's difficult to keep up my motivation at work. I am frustrated with my boss' repeated criticisms." When we don't use clear language, we can blow things out of proportion or have other people misunderstand what we're saying. Like reporters and detectives, we need to use clear language as well.

Separate facts from assumptions. When trying to be clear and objective in defining a problem, you may need to improve your own method of getting information by learning to separate out facts (accurate information) from assumptions. Being able to identify the facts minimizes the likelihood that judgments, assumptions, or misinterpretations that your mind has learned to make will interfere with your ability to be objective in defining the problem.

Assumptions are ideas that we take for granted as being true, yet may have no basis in actual fact. Although there are many types of assumptions, in order to illustrate how they work, we have broken down these assumptions into three types: fortune telling, doom seeking, and faulty reasoning.

Fortune telling occurs when you assume you know the future. Fortune telling assumptions are usually based upon similar situations that you've experienced or heard about from others. For example, suppose you experienced your parents' divorce as an extremely difficult emotional time. Now suppose that one of the things your parents constantly argued about was their different cultural backgrounds. Although you're missing many facts concerning the reasons for your parents' divorce, as an individual with this prior experience, you may find yourself fortune telling about relationships in general. For example, based upon your own history, you may find yourself forecasting that "mixed marriages never can work out. People marrying across cultures are in for a lot of pain." You're taking one factor from your past and projecting it absolutely on any similar future situations, regardless of differences that may exist.

Another common assumption, *doom seeking*, occurs when you make "what if?" statements in your head and assume that the worse-case scenario will happen. Such fearful assumptions can be enough to stop doom seekers from engaging in any further thinking about their question. For example, if you were trying to define the type of work you'd like to pursue, you may find yourself saying "But what if there is no work available that I'll enjoy?" You then extend this question to the assumption that this is indeed the case— you're *doomed* to a life situation in which you'll never enjoy your work.

Assumptions made through *faulty reasoning* are based upon taking a small amount of available information from one's past experiences and taking for granted that this situation defines *all* other instances. The thoughts with such assumptions often take the form of "if X happens, then Y will happen." The problem with faulty reasoning, similar to fortune telling, is that it's not based on repeated observations or proof of the facts.

What all of these assumptions have in common is that they are similar ways people have learned to think, but don't enable them to actually seek out the facts that can adequately test their assumptions. Yet, we all agree that seeking the facts and adequately testing assumptions is the best way to move science forward, make advances in business, medicine, and the law. Why not consider that this is the most effective way to define a personal problem as well? We provide tools in chapters 4 and 6 to help you "unlearn" the thoughts that you have learned to say to yourself over time. When you make assumptions and engage in this "automatic thought" process, you're not able to define problems clearly.

For example, let's say that two people both get a cold, bad-tasting cup of coffee in a restaurant. Both would agree that the coffee is cold—that is a fact. However, one might assume that the cold coffee was a mistake and no harm was intended. The other person might make the assumption that the restaurant owner was trying to save money and served them yesterday's coffee, not caring about the customers. Either one or both assumptions could be wrong. The only way to find out is to ask more questions and get the facts. Like detectives do when solving mysteries, problem solvers stick to the facts.

Identify what makes the situation a problem. Usually a problem occurs when a person is blocked in some way from getting what they want. This could be due to obstacles that are in the way, conflicting goals (ask any parent who has the goal of being a good parent and at the same time needs to earn an income for the family), reduced resources, recent changes, or actual losses.

Set realistic goals for changing the situation. This often means breaking down the problem into smaller parts so that you can set reachable goals and approach different parts of the problem one at a time.

Now write down the problem that you want to work on, remembering to:

❦ Gather all the facts,

❦ Use clear language,

❦ Separate facts from assumptions,

❦ Identify why the situation is a problem, and

❦ Set realistic goals for changing the situation.

Step 3: Brainstorm as Many Creative Ideas as Possible

Brainstorming involves making a list of as many possible alternatives or ideas to solve the problem as possible. It's important to write all of these ideas down. Even "silly" ideas should be written down, because they often lead to other ideas and good solutions.

There are only three rules for learning to creatively brainstorm, but they are very important ones.

Quantity is important. Generate as many ideas as possible. If you feel like your ideas are starting to dry up, start combining or making small changes to previous ideas. Another way to add to your list is to imagine how a very creative person or a role model might think. Remember the quote by Emile Cartier, "Nothing is more dangerous than an idea when it's the only one you have!"

Don't judge. When you're making a list of ideas, hold off criticizing them until you have completed your list. One sure way to stop your creative juices from flowing is to start to judge yourself before you even have a chance to get all your ideas down.

Think generally and specifically. Strategies are general ways of solving a problem, while tactics are specific means of carrying them out. For example, if you were generating a list of ideas about how you could make up with a friend following an argument, one strategy might be to arrange a time to talk to the friend to tell him that you're sorry. Different tactics of the same idea might include writing a letter, calling on the telephone, meeting for lunch, having another friend talk to him for you, and so on. Put all of these down on your list.

Now, using these brainstorming rules, write down a variety of possible solutions to the problem that you're working on.

Step 4: Decide What Solutions to Carry Out

Choose the ideas that are most likely to help you reach the goal that you set for yourself and the ideas that you're most likely to actually carry out. You can mark each idea with a rating of how likely they are to be effective and write some notes next to each alternative that you listed comparing the different consequences of each decision. Basically, you need to weigh the positive and negative consequences and determine which ideas come out better. It may be helpful to ask yourself the following questions when considering each alternative:

※ Can I actually carry out this idea? If not, what do I need to do to be able to do this?

※ Will this alternative meet my goals?

※ Will this alternative be likely to overcome obstacles?

※ What will be the consequences, both bad and good, of choosing this alternative?

❦ What will be the effect on myself, my values, or thoughts about myself if I choose this alternative?

❦ What will be the effect on people I care about if I choose this idea?

❦ What will be the short-term consequences?

❦ What will be the long-term consequences?

You will notice that some alternatives clearly have more advantages than others. Identify those that have better consequences as possible ideas to make up your solution plan.

Now, go back over each of the different solutions you just wrote down, and using the above criteria, rate each of the alternatives using a scale of 1 to 3, where 1 is not effective at all, 2 is moderately effective, and 3 is very effective.

Step 5: Develop a Plan and Carry Out Your Decision

Looking at the solutions with the highest ratings, or perhaps by combining two solutions to create an even more effective choice, develop a plan to carry out a highly rated solution. We all know that putting a plan into action can be hard to do, so it's important to write down your plan, and set a time limit for yourself to complete each step. Remember, the more specific tactics that make up your solution plan, the more likely it is that you will solve any problem.

If you need help in motivating yourself to carry out the plan, here are some suggestions to get you started:

❦ Make a list of all the consequences of not solving the problem and successfully solving the problem. This will keep you mindful of all your "good reasons" for putting a plan into action.

❦ Picture yourself carrying out the plan successfully. You may find it helpful to visualize what benefits you may experience if you're able to effectively improve this problem situation.

❦ Post a daily reminder with a slogan or personal motivation statement in a spot that you frequently see (for example, your refrigerator). We know one person who borrowed the "Just do it" slogan from Nike, stuck it on his refrigerator, and found it helpful as a useful reminder every time it caught his eye.

❦   Here's another inspirational quote that may be of help, this one by John F. Kennedy—" There are costs and risks to a program of action, but they are far less than the long-range risks and costs of comfortable inaction."

Step 6: Monitor Your Progress

Compare what you thought would happen with what actually happened. If the outcome was satisfactory, you know that you have successfully applied your problem-solving skills. If it wasn't, try again with a different problem, going through all the steps.

Reward yourself. Solving everyday problems is hard work! You should reward yourself for all the work that you put into this effort. Remember that it's especially important to reward yourself just for trying, not necessarily for finding the perfect solution or not having problems. As human beings, we will always have both day-to-day problems and major problems. Think about the long-term benefits to your life if you solve your day-to-day problems just 25 percent more effectively! Most people using the problem-solving tool report even more benefit than that.

Next, we provide a final tool, one that can enhance the longevity of your spiritual journey.

Create Your Spiritual Ritual

Many people attend some sort of religious services on a regular basis. Many people also observe religious rituals in their home, such as lighting Sabbath candles, creating a meditation altar or room, or preparing specific foods during certain religious holy days. Still other people have created rituals for themselves that focus on a quiet time for visualization, relaxation, and reflection. These include sitting and watching the ocean, taking a warm bath, listening to a CD of nature sounds, getting a massage, looking at the stars, or sitting in front of a fire. These rituals all provide different paths of sound, touch, and aroma, any of which can enhance our attention, relaxation, or spiritual experiences and keep us focused on our spiritual goals. Many of the activities in these rituals are part of complementary and alternative health-care services. Our reviews of the research into this area of health practice reveal support that such activities, such as those involving music, various aromas, or specific meditation activities, can actually stimulate parts of our brain that trigger a positive mood.

We believe that they are also an important part of awakening self-esteem because they provide a chance to give yourself a gift and a moment of appreciation for your own unique energy and vital essence. The last tool that we suggest in this book is to create your own spiritual ritual. It can be in your home, office, or yard, or it can be in a temple, mosque, shrine, cathedral, or place of nature. It may be something you read or say over and over to yourself, such as an affirmation or prayer. It may be a chance to engage in positive spiritual imagery such as breathing meditation or an awareness technique at a specific time each day. It may be an action as simple as washing your hands, symbolizing washing away the negative behavior, thoughts, or emotions that you have experienced throughout the day, or as complicated as studying ancient scriptures or philosophies. We provide a few samples below that were designed or shared with us by people we know, clients we have helped, or used ourselves at various points in time (anyone who has visited Art's university office has noticed the Zen water fountain that sits in the corner). Rituals can motivate us to tune in to the ongoing learning experiences we encounter on our continued journey.

The Candle Ritual

Light a candle for a brief ritual each morning and evening. Notice how the flame of the candle cannot be seen very clearly in the morning light. However, in the darkness, the light provides a warm glow and visible light. Take the time to reflect on how the candlelight is much like your LIFE or vital essence. Think about how, when things in your life are going along as planned, you may not need to focus on its light and energy or work to notice that part of yourself. However, in the dark or difficult times, the flame becomes an important source of warmth, light, and vision. Repeat an affirmation such as, "I will be conscious of the importance and strength of my inner flame."

The Music Ritual with Relaxation

Pick out a regular fifteen-minute period in which you select a record, CD, or tape to listen to. You can choose different music each time, but you should listen to the music as you sit or engage in a specific activity. This could be anything from breathing to the rhythm of the music, dancing, looking at your favorite photograph, or simply sitting with your eyes closed. Let your whole being experience appreciation for the moment.

The Reading Ritual

Take the opportunity to regularly read from inspirational texts. They can be anything from self-help books, such as this one, or inspirational stories, poems, or religious writings. After reading, write in your journal about how you could apply what you learned to your own life.

The Water Ritual

In a shower or bath, fill a cup of water and let it wash over your head, body, hands, or feet. As the water washes over you, be mindful of the warm and gentle flow of the water, and develop an affirmation about anything in your life that you wish to wash away and let dissolve. You'll be more tuned in to positive feelings and LIFE energy after such a ritual spiritual bath or shower, and you can focus in on them to enjoy them more.

The range and types of rituals we can describe are endless. We presented these rituals to give you a sample of the many ways in which people we know have created this ongoing gift to themselves. Try creating one for yourself.

Final Thoughts

Our inspiration for this book sprung from an insight that combining spiritual goals and psychological tools can provide a powerful way to awaken self-esteem. Spiritual awareness enlightens us to the assurance of our value as human beings and fosters our experience of joy, gratitude, and connection to others. Psychological tools traditionally focus on the "self-competence" part of self-esteem. This refers to helping us to think, feel, and act consistent with our spirituality or basic values. In order to do this, psychologists focus their energies on discovering and teaching people ways to increase their ability to understand, make decisions, relate to others, and cope with life. However, the cognitive-behavioral strategies developed through scientific study are often informed by historic spiritual and philosophical concepts. We have come to see the psychological and the spiritual as one big circle of the journey through life.

Spirituality Is Good for Us

Despite the many criticisms of specific religious systems or doctrine, the common spiritual bonds of love, acceptance, forgiveness, patience, and hope are good for us. When we act on these principles, our hearts and minds are open to receiving help and trying to solve difficult life challenges. Several years ago, we were made aware of the wealth of understanding and scientific investigations that have been compiled to document this. During a presentation at our Center for Behavioral Medicine and Mind/Body Studies by Dr. David Larson, then President of the National Institute for Healthcare Research, a summary of many of the studies was presented that further convinced us of the powerful force that is within us all.

Physician and scientist Andrew Newberg, who wrote *Why God Won't Go Away* along with coauthors Eugene D'Aquili and Vince Rause (2001), describe how the mysteries, beauty, and power of one's spirituality can be "life-transforming." We found their quoting of a section of the book, *Contact*, by Carl Sagan (1986), to be particularly poignant.

I was part of something wonderful, something that changes me forever; a vision of the universe that tells us undeniably how tiny, and insignificant, and how rare and precious we all are. A vision that tells us we belong to something that is greater than ourselves. That we are not, that none of us is, alone.

Our original *vision* was that this book would provide you with an affirmation of a basic and beautiful vital essence which you may have known was there, but overlooked on your previous quests for self-esteem.

Our *goal* was to provide some credible evidence that there are things that your mind has learned to say through years of conditioning that have blocked your spiritual journey and clouded your sense of self-esteem.

Our *objective* was to encourage you to make a personal commitment to change these thoughts and your reactions to them, the way you manage your feelings, the goals that you set for yourself, and the actions that you take to change.

Our *hope* is that your self-esteem has been awakened because your spiritual or moral beliefs confirm the knowledge that your LIFE is valuable and connected to all other LIFE. Through this book, you now have some tools to help you on the remainder of your life's journey. These tools, along with other tools you learn, can continue to increase your self-competence and self-esteem.

Remember the image of the large digital clock that we introduced in the first chapter? This clock may have led you to think about the length of your life and even your death. This isn't a bad thing to think about—in fact, we hear many stories of people who have been near death and survived that describe it as a "life-altering experience." They are no longer fearful to live life to the fullest degree possible. Let this book serve to awaken you to all you are meant to be! We end with a quote that celebrates life:

The mere sense of living is joy enough!

—Emily Dickinson

References

Baumeister, R F., E. Bratslavsky, C. Finkenauer, and K. D. Vohs. 2001. Bad is stronger than good. *Review of General Psychology* 5:323-370.

Beck, A. T. 1993. Cognitive therapy: Past, present, and future. *Journal of Consulting and Clinical Psychology* 61:194-198.

Brandon, N. 1992. *The Power of Self-Esteem: An Inspiring Look at Our Most Important Psychological Resource.* Deerfield Beach, FL: Health Communication, Inc.

Carlson, C. R., and R. H. Hoyle. 1993. Efficacy of progressive muscle relaxation training: A quantitative review of behavior medicine research. *Journal of Consulting & Clinical Psychology* 61:1059-1067.

Childre, D. L. 1994. *Freeze Frame, Fast Action Stress Relief.* Boulder Creek, CA: Planetary Publications.

Cotton, S. P., E. G. Levine, C. M. Fitzpatrick, K. H. Dold, and E. Targ. 1999. Exploring the relationships among spiritual well-being, quality of life, and psychological adjustment in women with breast cancer. *Psychooncology* 8:429-438.

Dickinson, E. 1976. *Complete Poems of Emily Dickinson.* NY: Little Brown & Co.

D'Zurilla, T. J., and A. M. Nezu. 1999. *Problem-Solving Therapy: A Social Competence Approach to Clinical Intervention.* 2d ed. New York: Springer.

Ellis, A. 2001. *Overcoming Destructive Beliefs, Feelings, and Behaviors: New Directions for Rational Emotive Behavior Therapy.* New York: Prometheus Books.

Enright, R. D. 2001. *Forgiveness Is a Choice: A Step-by-Step Process for Resolving Anger and Restoring Hope.* Washington, DC: American Psychological Association

Enright, R. D., and R. P. Fitzgibbons. 2000. *Helping Clients Forgive: An Empirical Guide for Resolving Anger and Restoring Hope.* Washington, DC: APA

Friedlander, Y., J. D. Kark, and Y. Stein. 1986. Religious orthodoxy and myocardial infarction in Jerusalem-a case control study. *International Journal of Cardiology* 10:33-41.

Goleman, D. 2003. Find happiness: Cajole your brain to lean to the left. *NY Times*, February 4.

Greenberger, D., and C. A. Padesky. 1995. *Mind over Mood: Change How You Feel by Changing the Way You Think.* New York: Guilford.

Hayes, S., K. Strosahl, and K. Wilson. 1999. *Acceptance and Commitment Therapy: An Experiential Approach to Behavior Change.* NY: Guilford Press

Jacobsen, E. 1938. *Progressive Relaxation.* Chicago: University Press

Kabat-Zinn, L. 1995. *Wherever You Go, There You Are: Mindfullness Meditation in Everyday Life.* New York: Hyperion.

Lewinsohn, P. M., R. Munoz, M. A. Youngsen, and A. M. Zeiss. 1978. *Control Your Depression.* New York: Simon and Schuster.

MacPhillamy, D. J., and P. M. Lewinsohn. 1982. The pleasant events schedule: Studies on reliability, validity, and scale intercorrelation. *Journal of Consulting and Clinical Psychology* 50: 363-380.

Marlatt, G. A., and J. L. Kristeller. 1999. Mindfulness and meditation. In *Integrating Spiraliry into Treatment: Resources for Practitioners,* edited by W. R. Miller. Washington, DC: American Psychological Association (pp. 67-84).

McCullough, M. E., R. A. Emmons, and J. Tsang. 2002. The grateful disposition: A conceptual and empirical topography. *Journal of Personality and Social Psychology* 82:112-127.

Miller, W. R., and J. C'de Baca. 2001. *Quantum Change: When Epiphanies and Sudden Insights Transform Ordinary Lives.* NY: Guilford Press.

Mueller, P. S., D. J. Plevak, and T. A. Rummans. 2001. Religious involvement, spirituality, and medicine: Implications for clinical practice. *Mayo Clinic Proceedings* 76:1225-1235.

Newberg, A., E. D'Aquili, and V. Rause. 2001. *Why God Won't Go Away.* NY: Ballantine Books.

Nezu, A. M., C. M. Nezu, and M. G. Perri. 1989. *Problem-Solving Therapy for Depression: Theory, Research, and Clinical Guidelines.* New York: Wiley.

Pennebaker, J. W. 1995. *Emotion, Disclosure, and Health.* Washington, DC: APA

Razali, S. M., C. I. Hasanah, K. Aminah, and M. Subramaniam. 1998. Religious-sociocultural psychotherapy in patients with anxiety and depression. *Australian and New Zealand Journal of Psychiatry* 32:876-872.

Sagan, C. 1986. *Contact.* NY: Pocket Books

Schnicke, M., and P. A. Resick. 1993. *Cognitive Processing Therapy for Rape Victims: A Treatment Manual.* Thousand Oaks, CA: Sage.

Seligman, M. E. P. 1998. *Learned Optimism: How to Change Your Mind and Your Life.* NY: Pocket Books.

Stetter, F., and S. Kupper. 2002. Autogenic training: A meta-analysis of clinical outcome studies. *Applied Psychophysiology & Biofeedback* 27:45-98.

Stone, A., J. M. Smith, A. Kaell, and A. Hurewitz. 2000. Structured writing about stressful events: Exploring potential psychological mediators of positive health effects. *Health Psychology* 19:619-624.

Snyder, C. R., S. S. Hardi, J. Cheavens, S. T. Michael, L. Yamhure, and S. Sympson. 2000. The role of hope in cognitive behavior therapies. *Cognitive Therapy and Research* 24:747-762.

Tix, A., and P. A. Frazier. 1998. The use of religious coping during stressful life events: Main effects, moderation, and mediation. *The Journal of Consulting and Clinical Psychology* 66:411-422.

Tolle, E. 1999. *The Power of Now: A Guide to Spiritual Enlightenment.* New World Library: Novato, CA.

Williamson, M. A. 2002. *Everyday Grace: Having Hope, Finding Forgiveness, and Making Miracles.* NY: Riverhead books.

Additional Notes

For more information on HeartMath's scientifically based techniques and research information visit their web site at www. Heartmath. com or write to them at:

HeartMath Institute
14700 West Park Avenue
Boulder Creek, CA 95006

Christine Maguth Nezu, Ph.D., ABPP, professor of psychology and associate professor of medicine at Drexel University, is codirector for the Center for Behavioral Medicine and Mind/Body Studies in Philadelphia, Pennsylvania. She is currently a Trustee for the American Board of Professional Psychology.

Arthur M. Nezu, Ph.D., ABPP, is past president of the Association for Advancement of Behavior Therapy (AABT) and currently professor of psychology, medicine, and public health at Drexel University. He is President of the American Board of Professional Psychology and codirector of the Center for Behavioral Medicine and Mind/Body Studies in Philadelphia, Pennsylvania.

E. Thomas Dowd, Ph.D., ABPP, is professor and interim chair of the Department of Psychology at Kent State University. He is a fellow of the American Psychological Association in two divisions.

Some Other
New Harbinger Titles

Survivng Your Borderline Parent, Item 3287 $14.95

When Anger Hurts, second edition, Item 3449 $16.95

Calming Your Anxious Mind, Item 3384 $12.95

Ending the Depression Cycle, Item 3333 $17.95

Your Surviving Spirit, Item 3570 $18.95

Coping with Anxiety, Item 3201 $10.95

The Agoraphobia Workbook, Item 3236 $19.95

Loving the Self-Absorbed, Item 3546 $14.95

Transforming Anger, Item 352X $10.95

Don't Let Your Emotions Run Your Life, Item 3090 $17.95

Why Can't I Ever Be Good Enough, Item 3147 $13.95

Your Depression Map, Item 3007 $19.95

Successful Problem Solving, Item 3023 $17.95

Working with the Self-Absorbed, Item 2922 $14.95

The Procrastination Workbook, Item 2957 $17.95

Coping with Uncertainty, Item 2965 $11.95

The BDD Workbook, Item 2930 $18.95

You, Your Relationship, and Your ADD, Item 299X $17.95

The Stop Walking on Eggshells Workbook, Item 2760 $18.95

Conquer Your Critical Inner Voice, Item 2876 $15.95

The PTSD Workbook, Item 2825 $17.95

Hypnotize Yourself Out of Pain Now!, Item 2809 $14.95

The Depression Workbook, 2nd edition, Item 268X $19.95

Beating the Senior Blues, Item 2728 $17.95

Call toll free, **1-800-748-6273,** or log on to our online bookstore at **www.newharbinger.com** to order. Have your Visa or Mastercard number ready. Or send a check for the titles you want to New Harbinger Publications, Inc., 5674 Shattuck Ave., Oakland, CA 94609. Include $4.50 for the first book and 75¢ for each additional book, to cover shipping and handling. (California residents please include appropriate sales tax.) Allow two to five weeks for delivery.

Prices subject to change without notice.